Our Daily Bread

Communication
as a Mission
and Ministry of the Church

Edited by
Karin Achtelstetter
in collaboration with Miriam Reidy Prost

on behalf of
The Lutheran World Federation – A Communion of Churches

Lutheran University Press
Minneapolis, Minnesota

Our Daily Bread –
Communication as a Mission and Ministry of the Church
Documentation No. 55, December 2010

Karin Achtelstetter, editor
in collaboration with Miriam Reidy Prost
on behalf of The Lutheran World Federation – A Communion of Churches

Translator: Anthony Coates
Editorial assistance: Libby Visinand and LWF Office for Communication Services
Design: LWF-OCS
Cover: © LWF/T. Rakoto

Published by Lutheran University Press under the auspices of:
The Lutheran World Federation
150, rte de Ferney, PO Box 2100
CH-1211 Geneva 2, Switzerland

Parallel edition in German available from Kreuz Verlag, Stuttgart, Germany
"Unser tägliches Brot – Kommunikation als Auftrag und Dienst der Kirche"

This book is also available in Europe under ISBN 978-2-940459-04-9

Library of Congress Cataloging-in-Publication Data

Our daily bread : communication as a mission and ministry of the church / Karin
Achtelstetter, editor.
      p. cm. -- (Documentation ; no. 55)
  ISBN-13: 978-1-932688-54-2 (alk. paper)
  ISBN-10: 1-932688-54-4 (alk. paper)
  1. Lutheran World Federation. 2. Communication--Religious aspects--Lutheran Church.
I. Achtelstetter, Karin, 1961-
  BX8004.L9O87 2010
  260.1'4--dc22

                        2010034879

Lutheran University Press, PO Box 390759, Minneapolis, MN 55439
Manufactured in the United States of America

Contents

Foreword

The Lutheran World Federation (LWF), its member churches and partner organizations have a long history of active involvement in developing communication skills and policies.

Today the role of communication in relation to the churches' self-understanding and programs is shifting. Discussion and sometimes controversy in recent decades can best be described as a pendulum swinging from communication as a mission and ministry of the church to communication as a public information service for the churches.

While the 1970s and 1980s emphasized communication as an integral part of the mission and ministry of the church, the 1990s saw a shift toward a service-oriented role within church administration, and therefore separate from the more specific proclamation of the gospel, education and advocacy. These changes were influenced by technological advances in communications and in society in general.

In 2009 the LWF organized an international consultation on "Communication: Our Daily Bread. Communication as a Mission and Ministry of the Church" at the Theological Faculty of the Friedrich-Alexander University in Erlangen, Germany. The meeting provided a platform where church communicators, policy makers, mission societies and other agencies could exchange information, discern new trends and discuss their expectations for communication in the churches in the 21st century.

The papers in this publication reflect the diversity and challenges to a communion of churches that seeks to affirm communication as a core feature of its identity.

Churches cannot talk about communion or about community in the biblical and theological sense without acknowledging the centrality of communication to the very birth of the Church itself. This is the message of Pentecost, to be kept in mind as Lutherans renew their fellowship.

Echoing the LWF Eleventh Assembly theme—as Lutherans we can say communication is our daily bread.

Rev. Dr Ishmael Noko
General Secretary
The Lutheran World Federation

Communication in the LWF – A Constructive Contradiction?

Karin Achtelstetter

1. From the Archives

1.1 In the beginning was the WORD …

> In the beginning was the WORD …

A history of the Lutheran World Federation (LWF) could start with this allusion to John 1:1.

While the LWF was still in the process of formation, its founders expressed their belief in the essential role of communication. In March 1946, more than a year before the LWF was founded in Lund (Sweden) in 1947, they established a news bulletin.

> This is the first edition of the "News Bulletin". By the Grace of God it may become an instrument of the Holy Spirit to give our great Lutheran Church her rightful place in the world. To strive for greater unity we must first get acquainted with each other. This is the first step in that direction.[1]

writes Sylvester Michelfelder, the bulletin's editor, who later became the first general secretary of the Federation.

Michelfelder does not talk about communication strategies but about the "Holy Spirit." Although he does not evoke visibility or branding, he talks about the "rightful place" of the Lutheran Church "in the world." Exchange of information is for him an essential part of the effort to reach greater unity.

Over the years, the place of communication within the LWF structure moved: at one time it was an Information Office, then a holistic—all-encompassing—Communication Department and then a service unit.

Despite the structural changes, some of the main challenges are still present and the major achievements are still relevant today. Let me mention just a few:

---

[1] Dr S.C. Michelfelder, *News Bulletin, Lutheran World Convention*, Vol. I, No.1, 15 March 1946.

Challenges:

- The language issue
- Active participation in information exchange between member churches
- Distribution and global public awareness

The language issue—I dare to say—has never been solved in a satisfactory way. And on distribution and public awareness, let me quote Communications director Hans Bolewski in his report to the Third LWF Assembly in Minneapolis (USA) in 1957: "There was a general complaint that our congregations, the man in the pew as well as the man in the street, knew little or nothing about the Federation, [and] that many did not understand why there should be a Lutheran ecumenical organization."[2]

Achievements:

- No matter how controversial the debates, there has always been reflection about communication and its relevance for the church within the LWF.

- The volume and quality of information—not only about the LWF secretariat, but especially about the life and work of the LWF member churches—is unusual for international ecumenical or confessional bodies. This was already highlighted in a proud report to the LWF assembly in Helsinki (Finland) in 1963: "It may be said that no other international Christian organization except the World Council of Churches and the Roman Catholic Church operates a global Christian news service of comparable scope, volume and frequency."[3]

1.2 Incarnational Communication as Constructive Contradiction

In preparation for this consultation, I have gone through documents that give testimony to more than 60 years of reflection, ideas, discussion, struggle and battle about the role of communication in a global Christian fellowship.

In fact, the title of this presentation is borrowed from a document I found in the LWF archives: the address of the chairman of the Committee on Communication (COC) at an LWF Executive Committee meeting that was to have

---

[2] Dr Carl E. Lund-Quist, ed., *Proceedings of the Third Assembly of the Lutheran World Federation*, Minneapolis, Minnesota, USA, August 15-25 1957 (Minneapolis: Augsburg Publishing House, 1958), 123.

[3] From the Communication Committee's report to the LWF Fourth Assembly in Helsinki in 1963 in *LWI* No. 24 (1996), 3.

taken place in Monrovia (Liberia) in 1980, but was actually held in Cartigny (Switzerland) due to the political situation in Liberia.

John W. Bachman was certainly an outstanding chairperson with regard to communication. With Bachman, the blooming LWF Communication Department had the professor of practical theology and the director of the Center for Communication and the Arts at Union Theological Seminary, New York as chairman. During his term of office, Communication became one of the Federation's four departments, thus attaining its highest-ever profile within the LWF structure.

The chairman of the Committee on Communication gave an almost programmatic speech about "Communication as Constructive Contradiction."

> We who operate from a Christian perspective do not expect to be completely at home in any structure, political or ecclesiastical. We will sense weakness in all systems, by whatever name, and reserve the right and obligation to call attention to them and to offer constructively contradictory options. We as communication specialists are not called upon to develop and document all of these options in political, socio-economic, and personal spheres, but we should offer guidance in the process through which the options receive consideration.[4]

Constructive contradiction, according to Bachman, has the two following elements: **internal involvement** and **interactive correction**. The prerequisites for communication as constructive contradiction are "a level of high trust among churches within the Federation" and "individuals who do trust and respect one another's Christian commitment."

Communication as constructive contradiction, again according to Bachman, is guided by the biblical concept of **stewardship**, which is an answer to the permanent struggle between the contradictory demands of individual freedom and social responsibility. He writes:

> As individuals we own nothing but have been granted everything both to enjoy and to share.[5]

Another recurrent theme in Bachman's thinking is his understanding of **incarnational communication**:

---

[4] Meeting of the LWF Committee on Communication, 16-24 April 1980, Monrovia, Liberia (meeting transferred to Cartigny, Switzerland). Exhibit 2.1, LWF/COC 1980 Agenda, Chairman's Address: *Communication as Constructive Criticism*.

[5] *Ibid.*

> The Christian Incarnation symbolizes a relationship which is much more conducive to communication. God in Christ has entered into human affairs, not imposing His will on persons but respecting individual integrity. He demonstrates the necessity of "participatory relationships" in communication but brings into the experience something from beyond. We are invited to follow Him in this precarious but exciting adventure.[6]

Hence, **incarnational communication** is an invitation to take risks. And "It is not simply asking life's questions but introducing a personal way of dealing with them. It is not embarrassed by the vertical dimension of the Christian faith."

Since the relationship of incarnation is based on identification with others, incarnational communication is working toward **reconciliation**.

1.3 Credible Communication – the Ecumenical Context

Bachman's addresses as chairman of the Committee (later Commission) on Communication make for fascinating reading. They testify to his creative reflection about communication as well as to his ability to introduce new and original terminology and concepts, which shaped not only the LWF's strategic thinking about communication, but also the way communication was implemented within the Federation.

Of course, the LWF's increased interest in and emphasis on communication in the late '70s and '80s was not an isolated phenomenon. The Sixth Assembly of the World Council of Churches (WCC) in 1983 in Vancouver (Canada) emphasized the need for **credible communication**:

> Credible communication serves the cause of justice and peace by setting standards that resist national, cultural, racial stereotypes and the building of enemy images, and provide space and time for the views of minority and marginalized groups.[7]

2. Changing World, Changing Paradigms – the "Tipping Point"

From this brief overview, you may already sense the historical and political background behind this account of LWF Communication history: the Cold

---

[6] *Ibid.*

[7] David Gill, ed., *Gathered for Life: Official Report, VI Assembly World Council of Churches, Vancouver, Canada, 24 July-10 August 1983* (Geneva: WCC Publications, 1983), 106.

War, individual and collective human rights concerns and the ecumenical movement's anti-apartheid struggle.

These events and concerns shaped the thinking about communication and its role in the international church organizations as well as in many national churches in the '70s and '80s.

The international church organizations, fighting for the rights of those who had no voice in the public sphere and providing platforms of encounter and dialogue between those who were separated by the Iron Curtain, entered the public sphere and caught media attention with authentic and transparent communication rather than with sophisticated public relations and marketing strategies.

2.1 Witnessing the Changes

I have invited several witnesses *(Zeitzeugen)* to comment on this period:

Charles M. Austin (English editor, LWF, 1976-1979):

> Among the continuing discussions and sometimes controversies was the relationship between communications policies in the church and the news-gathering and news-reporting practices in the secular world. [...] When I began work in church news media in 1972, it was alongside a number of men and women who [...] continually fought for the "independence" of the church journalist and the policy of telling the truth and issuing news releases that met the standards of secular journalism. [...] Our job was to write the news and disseminate it in ways that would be useful to the secular media. This meant using a certain style and crafting our stories a certain way. Before my tenure as English editor for the Lutheran World Federation—1976-1979—men like William Dudde and Neil Mellblom had brought this viewpoint into the LWF. But there were some who were chipping away at the independence of the information bureau and felt it should be more tightly controlled. They wanted to withhold information (even if the information was "out there" in other ways) or to regulate its release to meet bureaucratic or egotistical purposes.[8]

Jonathan Frerichs (Consultative Services, LWF, 1982-1990):

> In the '70s and '80s, communication was "daily bread" for the LWF in its international mission. There was a varying mix between "mission" and "development," to use those terms. The strongest heritage was in mission but the pull was toward development and justice. [...] The time I was at LWF [...] was a kind of tipping

---

[8] Charles M. Austin, unpublished (private communication to author), 2009.

point. There was extensive engagement with "global issues" and there was also narrower, institutional communication work including publications and some very limited promotion of the LWF itself. [...] the "biggest" thinking was in the justice-related work and in communication development seen from that perspective. This was the era of UNESCO, the "New World Information and Communication Order" and the MacBride Report *Many Voices One World*. Debating, deciding and assessing LWF's role was shaped by the partnership with the World Association for Christian Communication (WACC) and with WCC Communication. The communication desk at the *Evangelisches Missionswerk* (EMW) Hamburg was also a key player for LWF and WACC. [...] All shared the interest in communication development that was, essentially, for social justice.[9]

The ecumenical movement and, thus, the international church organizations, were associated with social justice issues, the anti-racism struggle, disarmament and bridge-building.

The early '90s were a "tipping point," as Jonathan Frerichs put it, in the self-understanding of the LWF as well as with regard to global geopolitical developments. Let us hear two more witnesses:

Roger R. Kahle (English editor of Lutheran World Information, LWF, 1979-1987):

When I arrived at the LWF headquarters in August of 1979 no one was there! That's not quite true. But most [...] were attending the LWF Executive Committee meeting in Brazil. The hot topic at that meeting was "ecclesial density," which was a "dense" way of saying, "What is the LWF?" Just a bunch of Lutheran churches or something more? When I left the LWF a little more than eight years later that question had been answered [...] The answer was: "communio"—a communion of faith. During those eight years I witnessed the strong development of that sense of communion.[10]

Anneli Janhonen (director & editor-in-chief, Office for Communication Services, LWF, 1992-1998):

When I [...] began my work as the director/editor-in-chief of the LWF Office for Communication Services, I was soon asked by the general secretary to prepare for the Council a proposal to discontinue the Lutheran minority churches' information

---

[9] Jonathan Frerichs, unpublished (private communication to author), 2009.

[10] Roger R. Kahle, unpublished (private communication to author), 2009.

service IDL. This service had been operating for years from Budapest and later from Vienna. I did not quite foresee what kind of a mine was hidden in this plan. [...]

Anyway, the IDL was closed to the deep disappointment and anger of communicators and church leaders from the East European region in particular, but also from other German-speaking churches. It took years to calm down the disappointment. It was as if the reasons for the closing of the service were not fully understood. The main reason for this painful action was that the fall of the Soviet Union and the Berlin wall had abolished barriers to the free flow of information. The second reason was that the decreasing funds of the Federation were badly needed to improve communication services in the less privileged parts of the Lutheran communion, particularly in Africa. And the strengthening of communion was to be the main goal of the LWF.

The closing of the IDL was—at least to some extent—compensated for by creating a network of correspondents in the minority churches in Europe, with the precious support of KALME. This pattern was also implemented successfully later in African and Asian churches.

At the same time, with the closing of the IDL, the process to launch *Ecumenical News International* (*ENI*) was proceeding. One of the most important, positive actions the LWF has ever taken in the field of communication was to be a co-sponsor of *ENI*. This was a right move although it meant restrictions in the financial resources of the LWF's own communication services. With this decision and the annual granting of funds, the LWF´s leadership showed a deeper understanding of the role of communication in the mission of the Church universal. It showed also that the LWF wanted to be truly ecumenical, not only in words but also in deeds.[11]

These four comments show quite nicely how the role of communication in the LWF evolved during the '70s, '80s and '90s in response to developments and challenges in the global political and ecumenical context. In this evolution, we can distinguish three periods, each with its particular emphasis:

- professionalization of church journalism, which meant open and honest reporting on activities ('70s);

- emphasis on the prophetic role of communication in overcoming political, economic and cultural barriers ('80s);

---

[11] Anneli Janhonen, unpublished (private communication to author), 2009.

- focus on communication interpreting the Lutheran communion, strengthening its growth, supporting the formation of global and regional (Lutheran) identity and expressions as well as fostering the mission of the Church universal ('90s).

2.2 Communication and Communio

"How to Interpret the Lutheran Communion" was the programmatic title of an international consultation that took place in Geneva in 1995. The title successfully evokes the overall orientation of LWF communication activities in the '90s.

The aim of the 1995 consultation was "to find together ways of how better to communicate the Lutheran communion—the LWF and its member churches—to their own constituency and to the public, and how to improve member churches' mutual communication and information exchange."

In their reflections, the participants observed that:

> The tendency in the churches—and in their communication—is to go from the global to the regional and local. But in order to make the worldwide Lutheran communion real, a global view is necessary. Building global awareness is an important task of the churches' communicators. This does not happen simply by bringing international news home but by making global events relevant at the local level. Global awareness is created locally [...][12]

At the same event, LWF general secretary Rev. Dr Ishmael Noko described the role of communication in the LWF as

> [...] a process of binding people together into one. When information is shared and thoughts and ideas exchanged, different cultures meet and are bound together. [...] Sharing burdens and caring for one another are the key to communication and communion and the communicator is called to nurture the life of people, of churches and communities.[13]

The self-reflection/growing self-awareness *(Selbstbesinnung)*, the focus on LWF identity and hence, Communication's role in supporting these self-definition processes, can only be understood in the context of world geopolitical changes and a radical shift of paradigms in the '90s. While communication in the '80s

---

[12] Report of a Consultation on "How to interpret the Lutheran Communion," 1-4 March 1995, Geneva, Switzerland, 7.

[13] *Ibid.* 11.

was clearly directed toward the civil society and secular world, communication in the '90s appears to have been more inward-looking.

As a logical consequence, the more prophetic role of **constructive contradiction** (as Bachman would call it) found its expression in the Office for International Affairs and Human Rights, while social justice development-related communication programs and projects found a new home in the Department for Mission and Development (DMD) where, however, regional communication needs were a greater priority. As a result, the Ecumenical Advocacy Alliance (EAA) was created with responsibility for the more advocacy-related forms of communication; the LWF is an active member of EAA.

The *Guiding Principles for Comprehensive Communication – A Communicative Communion* which were brought to the LWF Council in 2002 are a result of this self-reflection and identity-building process.

This document's Mission and Vision Statements bring this clearly to light:

LWF Communication Mission

The LWF, a communion of churches, is inspired by God's love for all creation and shaped by its communication. The role of LWF communications is to ensure standards and facilities that enable effective communication processes to promote, develop and sustain this communion.

LWF Communication Vision

In the LWF, communication creates, gives expression to and strengthens a just, inclusive and participatory communion reaching out to shape the abundant life promised by Christ, part of every human being's daily experience.

This vision, this dream for the future, can be briefly described as: "The LWF: A Communicative Communion."[14]

2.3 LWF Communication between Aspiration and Reality

While the *Guiding Principles for Comprehensive Communication* was in its final drafting stages, the LWF Council in 2001 asked the LWF general secretary to appoint a task force on communication[15] with the following mandate:

- to critically analyze the OCS Terms of Reference in light of the service the office provides to (i) the LWF member churches, (ii) Geneva Secretariat Structure, (iii) ecumenically and (iv) to the public at large;

---

[14] Meeting of the LWF Council, Wittenberg, Germany, 10-17 September 2002, Exhibit 16.1, 6.

[15] Minutes of the Meeting of the LWF Council, 12-19 June 2001, Geneva, Switzerland, 30.

- to review LWF structures, including its related agencies, where communication is lodged, i.e., in the LWF Department for Mission and Development
and its related structures in LWF regions, *Ecumenical News International*
and the Communication office of Action for Churches Together …[16]

The task force promoted a more holistic understanding of communication, encompassing:

- the importance of a proactive role for communication;
- the need to speak to both internal and external communication;
- the public relations responsibility;
- the inclusion of fund-raising and advocacy,
- acknowledging at the same time that the present Terms of Reference of the Office for Communication Services as well as its structure did not allow for this broader, more inclusive understanding.

2.3.1 Enhancing Communication, Mutual Accountability and Sharing

As an outcome of the LWF Tenth Assembly in 2003 in Winnipeg (Canada) and the subsequent Strategic Planning process in the LWF Secretariat, "Enhancing Communication, Mutual Accountability and Sharing" was identified as one of the four LWF Priority Areas. Acknowledging its specific role, this became a cross-cutting priority:

> The LWF as a living system needs to address "the enhancement of communica-
> tion, mutual accountability and sharing" […] in each of the priority areas and
> the associated directions and programmatic goals. These dimensions are deeply
> rooted in the programmatic work and cannot exist independently. Mutual ac-
> countability and sharing are qualities that describe the ethos of communication
> and interaction within the communion. Thus, this cross-cutting priority chal-
> lenges the LWF continually to question, critically assess, and improve patterns
> of interaction in all its programmatic activities.[17]

Although no structural changes were introduced, the attempt to reach a more holistic understanding of communication, accountability and sharing is apparent within the Secretariat. Other actions and activities point in the same direction.

---

[16] "Task Force on Communication Report to the General Secretary." Meeting of the LWF Council, Wittenberg, Germany, 10-17 September 2002, Exhibit 16.2, 1.

[17] *Living in Communion in the World Today*, Documentation 52 (Geneva: LWF, 2007), 214.

2.4. From Interpreting the Communion to Authentic Communication. Concepts and Expressions of the Communion

At its 2004 meeting, the LWF Council voted to carry out a **comprehensive communication audit** of LWF unit publications and Web sites as well as a summary of what is currently available in print and via the Web sites.

As a result of this audit, the OCS started various pilot projects, ensuring the involvement of LWF regions in production and distribution, worked on audience identification and targeting, and invested in Web development.

Last year's Roundtable on the Development of a Web site for the Lutheran Communion clearly indicated that a new decade in communication has dawned. Rather than asking how communication can **interpret** the Lutheran communion, strengthen its growth and support the formation of global and regional (Lutheran) identity, the emphasis was on finding **new and authentic concepts and expressions of communication** which reflect the communion's self-understanding as **spiritual, sacramental, confessional, witnessing and serving**.

The shift is clearly from interpretation to authentic expressions of communication.

Is this the vision for the future or just a reference to the recent past?

As we approach the Eleventh LWF Assembly under the theme "Give Us Today Our Daily Bread," how do we envisage communication in a renewed Lutheran World Federation, in a communion of churches? What is the message we want to give to the Renewal Committee, which will present its report to the LWF Council meeting in October this year?

What is our vision for renewed communication?

Let me conclude with two messages:

The Program Committee for Communication addressed the following message to the Renewal Committee at the Council meeting in Arusha (Tanzania) in 2008:

> The Program Committee for Communication Services (PCCS) discussed the report of the Renewal Committee and **welcomed** the proposal to cluster communication and advocacy, as this would ensure more action and campaign-oriented communication and thus enhance the LWF's visibility.
>
> It however expressed **concern** about the broad thematic orientation, i.e. women and youth etc.
>
> It **regretted** that the proposed structural changes do not address—at all—the existing, inefficient and counterproductive division of communication services and communication projects and programs. A communion which is growing together needs a holistic and strategic approach to communication. Therefore communication should not be split into program and service-related activities.

It is the conviction of the committee that the way in which the LWF communicates needs to be an authentic expression of its self-understanding as a communion of churches.

It therefore **challenges** the Renewal Committee in view of a more holistic approach to communication

- to also include the task of fund-raising in the tasks of the proposed cluster
- to bring together program, project and service-oriented communication activities;
- to consider renaming this cluster PUBLIC ISSUES (instead of Global issues). [...][18]

And Jonathan Frerich's reflections:

In the '90s it became possible for churches and related ministries to do more things bilaterally and they did. There was less power, less talent and fewer resources made available for multilateral instruments like the LWF, the WCC and WACC. The same trend continues today, but now there is a new opportunity:

Will the churches address global issues that do not respect borders and will not be solved by national or denominational initiatives?

What are these global challenges? Which ones require a church response for the sake of the gospel? What could churches do about the chosen challenges, together?

With strong common will, communication could easily "serve" these global causes. Without that commitment, no amount of technology or talent will suffice. To put it positively, the international community must begin to work for certain "global common goods" such as climate control, poverty reduction and peace-building on a scale that surpasses what was needed to meet past challenges that were less "global" in nature. Churches guided by the Holy Spirit could "serve" that goal from their unique place in society—as Christians, with other faiths and with civil society as appropriate and necessary. In communications and other relevant disciplines, this is an opportunity to apply the lessons of recent decades to a mission fit for the 21st century.

Why have I chosen Bachman's concept of communication as **constructive contradiction** for this presentation?

Because it is in this spirit that communication and organizations can advance; and I hope that this spirit will lead us in this consultation process.

[18] The Lutheran World Federation, *Proceedings, Program Committee for Communication Services*, Arusha, Tanzania, 2008, 8-9.

On Communication – Intercultural Comparison or Intercultural Encounter

Andreas Nehring

Over the next three days, we shall be reflecting on various aspects of communication as a mission of the Church or the churches. We wish to discuss different or common expectations of the role and place of communication in the mission and ministry of churches in the 21st century.

But before we go into the details, I would like to raise some theoretical points of interest.

Communication seems to be a major concern of the Lutheran communion, but its role and place in relation to the churches' self-understanding and actions has still to be debated. I believe that one reason for the different approaches to concepts of church communication is rooted in cultural differences and contextually different self-understandings of what the church is or how church identity is conceptualized. Before we discuss how to implement communication strategies on a practical level and begin work on understanding our policy-making in relation to communication and the mission of the churches, I would like to step back for a moment and share with you some reflections on what seems to be fundamental for this conference: the question of hermeneutics in intercultural encounter.

We all come from culturally different backgrounds. Intercultural hermeneutics is concerned with the understanding of the culturally other, and its subject area is the interaction between members of different cultures. How do we analyze this interaction? What theoretical implications does reflection on these interactions as mediated communication strategies have? What is communication in relation to culture? What is the role of language as the still dominant medium for communication?

The relationship of one's own to a foreign language generally serves as a pattern for the exchange between one's own and another culture. Epistemologically, intercultural hermeneutics faces the problem that the other culture cannot just be understood as an aberration of one's own! Culture generates its meaningfulness by its own performance. Cultures are not given entities but are differentiated out of themselves, and are self-referential at least in the sense that they are different. They cannot, therefore, be compared like objects. What is missing is a transcendent point of view that would allow comparison. At least in this line of reflection, intercultural hermeneutics faces the theoretical and epistemological problem that encounter situations cannot be levelled by an explicit *tertium comparationis*.

What I can do in this paper is exclude practical questions of people encountering one another, and ask whether and how we can identify common ground between members of different cultures. The reflection on intercultural encounter is deeply affected by hermeneutical differentiation between self- and other-ness on the one hand, and understanding and misunderstanding on the other.

The German philosopher Werner Kogge identified three areas of hermeneutical concern related to the question of cultural difference:

- the perceptibility of different cultures;
- the universality and rationality of validity claims; and
- the possibilities of practical communication with the other or with strangers.[1]

The rich tradition of intercultural theology has a lot to say on all these issues, but today, I will focus only on the first and third aspects of Kogge's argument.

Kogge admits that if intercultural philosophy considers these issues, it often deals only with the first two, while intercultural encounter usually focuses on the last point. It seems to me that in the field of ecumenical as well as inter-religious dialogue, the second and third points are the main focus. While the so-called "theology of religions" in general deals with the question of the universality and rationality of validity claims, ecumenical work since the 1980s on "dialogue in community" has been more and more involved in practical questions of encounter; the perceptibility of another culture is more or less taken for granted or dealt with on the basis of relatively traditional premises of hermeneutics. Until now therefore, the hermeneutic approach has been dominant in theological reflections on inter-religious encounters.

Deriving from a tradition of interpreting historically different texts and the attempt to adequately grasp their meaning, intercultural hermeneutics from the very beginning has also emphasized the importance of the historical and cultural context for a proper understanding of the other. In recent years, hermeneutics in scholarly discourse is nevertheless more and more in decline, and it seems to lack any relevance for work on actual questions in a globalized world. The emphasis has shifted from understanding to the question of the perceptibility of different cultures. Contexts have become shaky and fluid; cultural identities have become "constructed" and thus questionable. And with these growing post-modern insecurities, the epistemological basis for the perception of contexts has become questionable as well.

---

[1] Werner Kogge, *Grenzen des Verstehens: Kultur-Differenz-Diskretion* (Weilerswist: Velbrück Verlag, 2002), 25.

The Perceptibility of Different Cultures

Whereas in theology, cross-cultural encounter is mainly considered within the perspective of ecumenical and inter-religious dialogues, a discourse model has become prominent in the field of cultural studies over the past 25 years. This model was appropriated by Edward Said in his attempt to reveal the power structure of Western influence in colonial contexts. With reference to Michel Foucault and Antonio Gramsci, Said has argued that European orientalism has not only represented oriental cultures in science, literature and art, but at the same time has exerted power over the Orient. These two kinds of reflection have hardly intersected until now. Many of the traditional theological presuppositions on the perception of the culturally and religious other have no doubt been critically analyzed.[2] Inter-religious dialogue and some aspects of intercultural hermeneutics, outlined in comparative studies for the understanding of the other,[3] have also been discussed theologically.[4] However, the fact that the conditions for comprehension are linked to power and set by hegemonic discourse has hardly been taken into consideration in current ecumenical dialogues.

For a long time, one of the central theoretical concerns of colonial discourse theory was representation and the political implications of representing the colonized in anthropology, religious studies, literature and even art. The other line of theoretical reflection is related to anti-colonial resistance, counter-discourses, pre-colonial knowledge, knowledge subjugated in the dominant discourse, the agency of the colonized, subaltern consciousness etc. In both fields, the question of subjectivity or the position of the subject is at stake; for further theoretical interventions in the field of colonial discourse—historically oriented as well as concerned with the present—the question of how these subject positions are constructed seems to be relevant. While during the 1960s and '70s, academic concern focused predominantly on the social aspects of intercultural encounter, post-colonial studies since the 1980s have shifted the emphasis of critique to a

---

[2] The literature on this is widely scattered; see, for example, Michael Mildenberger (ed.), *Denkpause im Dialog. Perspektiven der Begegnung mit anderen Religionen und Ideologien* (Frankfurt a.M.: Lembeck, 1978); Reinhold Bernhardt, *Der Absolutheitsanspruch des Christentums. Von der Aufklärung bis zur Pluralistischen Religionstheologie* (Gütersloh: Gütersloher Verlagshaus, 1993).

[3] Alois Wierlacher (ed.), *Kulturthema Fremdheit. Leitbegriffe und Problemfelder kulturwissenschaftlicher Forschung* (München, 1993); Bernhard Waldenfels, *Der Stachel des Fremden* (Frankfurt a.M.: Suhrkamp, 1990); Henning Wrogemann, *Mission und Religion in der systematischen Theologie der Gegenwart* (Göttingen: Vandenhoek und Ruprecht, 1997).

[4] Theo Sundermeier, *Den Fremden verstehen. Eine praktische Hermeneutik* (Göttingen: Vandenhoek und Ruprecht, 1996); *Was ist Religion? Religionswissenschaft im theologischen Kontext* (Gütersloh: Gütersloher Verlagshaus, 1999); Andreas Grünschloss, *Der eigene und der fremde Glaube. Studien zur interreligiösen Fremdwahrnehmung in Islam, Hinduismus, Buddhismus und Christentum* (Tübingen: Mohr, 1999).

deconstruction of colonial knowledge and its underlying assumptions. The focus of attention has moved from social aspects to the question of culture.[5]

Critique of Hermeneutics

This shift has led to a critique of hermeneutics as well.

Trained in the reading of texts, hermeneutics has failed in the eyes of many to explain cultural differences. One of the main points of critique is that hermeneutics focuses mainly on the articulated contents of oral or written expressions. But the structural conditions of understanding—like power structures, dominant representations of cultural identity, the economic and political conditions in which thoughts are articulated, and the whole area of the ideological interpellation of people who speak—are neglected.

Another critique of hermeneutics holds that the perception of culture is mostly confined to text and interpretation, and that culture thereby is considered as synonymous with texts. What is necessary is a wider concept of culture that perceives it not first and foremost as a normatively coined complex of cultural products, but as a coded network of constructions and negotiations of meaning.

What is required is reflection on how interpretations are constituted and reconstituted inter-subjectively, and how the parties involved adjust to one another in their interpretations. These adjustments afford openings for conflict, power struggles and hegemonic counter-discourses; they are interwoven into the histories of colonial or post-colonial dominance and structures of dependency.[6]

In many societies, "Cultural Turns"[7] have led to a shift in the understanding of culture over the past 20 years as a predominantly mental affair and a moment of representation to that of culture as a dynamic product and force of human activity and social practices.

It can be argued that this anti-essentialist characterization of culture, as discussed above in brief, is a result of a wide innovative theoretical shift. "Cultures," James Clifford has maintained, "do not hold still for their portraits. Attempts to make them do so always involve simplification and exclusion, selection of a temporal focus..."[8] This widespread analytical conviction has informed a variety of

---

[5] Nicholas Thomas, *Colonialism's Culture: Anthropology, Travel and Government* (Princeton: Princeton University Press, 1994).

[6] Eberhard Berg and Martin Fuchs, "Phänomenologie der Differenz, Reflexionsstufen ethnographischer Repräsentation", in: Eberhard Berg and Martin Fuchs, eds, *Kultur, Soziale Praxis, Text. Die Krise der ethnographischen Repräsentation* . (Frankfurt/Main: Suhrkamp 1993), 11-109.

[7] Cf. Doris Bachmann-Medick, *Cultural Turns. Neuorientierungen in den Kulturwissenschaften*, (Hamburg: Rowohlt Taschenbuch, 2006).

[8] James Clifford and George E. Marcus, eds, *Writing Culture. The Poetics and Politics of Ethnography* (Berkeley: University of California Press, 1986), 10.

theoretical attempts to analyze the intercultural encounter as hybrid, unbounded, as "in-between" spaces and the like. There is nevertheless a theoretical as well as practical problem in this emphasis on the fluidity of culture in post-modern/post-colonial contexts. The view of culture as fluid seems best to serve the post-modern theorizers in Western academia, but it rarely matches with the self-estimation of those who were forced to establish new or transformed identity positions in their respective contexts. The essentialization of cultural identity as original, divinely created, national, racial, and the like is widespread not only among fundamentalists but also among a wide range of cultural agents on almost all continents.

Religion especially seems to be a vital force in this contest for identity positions in all postcolonial contexts. The emphasis on hybridity or fluidity as tools for the analysis of intercultural encounters thus seems insufficient. How are cultural identities formed? By what means are identity positions convincingly formulated? How do intercultural encounters influence the formulation of identity positions? How are subject positions questioned? What is the role of religions vs. ideologies in the formulation of subject positions? What is the role of language as a means to formulate subject positions? Questions related to the ambivalence of freedom are at stake. The spontaneity of an individual expression or a subjective interpretation is always linked to the limitations of tradition. I think a lot of theological reflection still remains to be done in this field.

What I have discussed so far is in many ways related to a more abstract concern with the role of language and of texts. And this is especially important for any reflection on communication. Words do not only name, describe and judge but also produce, constitute or create reality. Edward Said has called this relationship of reality and text "the worldliness of a text." We can ask how words, like the texts we produce, constitute the reality they describe. How do they function? Said has reflected on this question in his theoretical essay, "The World, the Text and the Critic," in which he pointed out that every text is a text-in-the-world. According to Said, all texts are worldly, "[...] even when they appear to deny it, they are nevertheless part of the social world, human life, and of course the historical moments in which they are located and interpreted."[9]

Critique of Communication

We should bear in mind that the massive critique faced by hermeneutical approaches is accompanied by an equally strong attack on theories of inter-cultural communication. The Slovenian philosopher Slavoj Žižek, for example,

---

[9] Edward Said, *Die Welt, der Text und der Kritiker* (Frankfurt a.M.: Fischer Verlag, 1997), 11. (Original: *The World, the Text, and the Critic*, Cambridge: Cambridge University Press, 1983).

has criticized the idea of a hegemonic free discourse (as expounded by Jürgen Habermas) that also serves as a role model for many reflections on dialogue in an ecumenical context in which communication as an ideal speech act has become a fetish. Although Habermas would recognize that communication is often broken and distorted, he nevertheless insists that reason, ethics and democracy can be grounded on this assumed ideal speech act situation, and that as soon as we enter a situation of communication, we should presuppose an ideal of unbroken communication in order to be able to communicate at all.

By doing so, Žižek argues, Habermas is resorting to an ideological masking of the ultimate failure of the social to constitute an all-encompassing space of representation.[10] This seems relevant for some of the discussions at our conference. Despite all the acknowledged failures of speech acts in situations of inter-religious or intercultural encounter and communication, ecumenical dialogues are based at least theoretically on the assumption that they take place in an all-encompassing cultural or social space, even if we are aware of cultural and religious differences within other cultures.

We do not only dialogue with Catholics or Baptists, but with Catholics who speak, for example, from their context in Rwanda, or with Baptists from Nagaland in North India, or with other Lutherans from culturally different contexts than our own. Again, it is the existence of a homogeneous cultural space, a space that at least theoretically is able to harmonize antagonisms, that is in question here.

Besides Žižek, many others have contributed to an ongoing deconstruction of culture, context and text as perceptible entities. In his groundbreaking article "Signature, Event, Context," Jacques Derrida argued that if we take it for granted that the broad field covered by the word "communication" is limited by what is called "context," then it must be asked whether "the prerequisites of a context [are] ever absolutely determinable." In this article, Derrida demonstrates why determination of a context can never be certain or exhaustive.[11] For Derrida, questioning the stability of context implies an adjustment in the conceptualization of Scripture or writing—that has traditionally been seen as a medium of communication, "at least if communication is understood in the restricted sense of the transmission of meaning."[12]

Communication is not the process of transmission of a word or text from sender to receiver which thereby has gone through the mill of hermeneutic scrutiny. Rather,

---

[10] Slavoj Žižek, "Jenseits der Diskursanalyse," in: Oliver Marchart (hg.), *Das Undarstellbare der Politik. Zur Hegemonietheorie Ernesto Laclaus* (Wien: Turia und Kant, 1998), 123–131. Cf.: Jacob Torfing, *New Theories of Discourse: Laclau, Mouffe and Žižek*, (Oxford, UK & Malden, Mass.: Blackwell Publishers, 1999), 11.

[11] Jacques Derrida, "Signature, Event, Context." In Jacques Derrida, *Margins of Philosophy*, (Chicago: University of Chicago Press, 1982), 310.

[12] Derrida, *Margins of Philosophy*, 310.

the spoken word or written text can be taken out of its own, or better, out of any context and grafted onto another. The power of any speech act lies neither in its conventional use nor in the traditional setting from which it supposedly comes, but in the possibility of a break with the context, and whether the utterance or text can be cited or reiterated. If a text or utterances function and have power only because they are repeatable and thereby deferrable, then it is no longer the intentionality of the speaker or the decipherable de-contextualized meaning of the utterance or text that interests us. Rather, meaning is generated in the performance of speech acts. As I have already indicated, these questions are important for all reflections on intercultural theology as well as on ecumenical dialogue.

Possibilities of Practical Communication with Strangers

An equally important point in relation to intercultural encounter and ecumenical dialogue is that of possibilities of practical communication with strangers. If we do not deny that cultures can perhaps be measured by the same standards and if, at the same time, we admit that the other culture cannot be translated completely into our own cultural patterns, then we must reflect on what members of two different cultures may have in common. The suggestion that two cultures are incommensurable or that there is an untranslatable otherness between the two has at least to be based on experience. Even the experience of partial untranslatability must refer to some accessibility that transcends the cognitive comparison of two different cultural elements. If we say that something cannot be translated, that does not mean that it cannot be compared. If we claim that there is no equivalent for our concept in the other culture or language, we have to have at least a point of comparison, even if this point cannot be expressed in either of the compared cultures. The comparison, which is intentional, transcends any explicit articulation precisely because it is based on the reflection that it has to refer to implicit contents that cannot be expressed between cultures but are present in practical or common usage.

Implicit and Explicit Knowledge
Erlangen sociologist Joachim Renn has therefore suggested that if

- we don't want to fall into the puzzle of cultural incommensurability;
- we continue to try to cope with the experience of un-translatability; and
- we try to express what the results of the discovery of the limits of one's own identity in the comparison of cultures are,

- then we must make a distinction between performative and explicit culture. And this applies equally to religious culture. We have to differentiate between religious experience and performance on the one hand, and religious doctrines, texts or ritual expressions on the other. Both can be distinguished from one another by the role and function of explicit language.

Most of the conceptualizations of culture follow a basically cognitive model. Culture is explicit culture, considered to be a system of knowledge based on intentionality, a symbolic system based on a linguistic and textual structure or an institutional system based on norms and values. The decisive systematic issue in relation to intercultural encounter and translation is, as Joachim Renn emphasizes, the need to understand this explicit articulation of culture in terms of knowledge, typologies and linguistic patterns as an act of translation as well.

The transition from implicit knowledge to explicit articulation is to be seen as a translation. Cultural knowledge thereby undergoes an important shift. The erroneous character of any **cognitivist** concept of culture is that it assumes that implicit knowledge is a complete representation of deeply rooted cultural knowledge that simply has not been made explicit so far. Renn makes very clear that explicit formulation of culture is not only an abstraction of lived cultural experience but also, necessarily, a process of selection in which much of the implicit content is lost, and which can never be an adequate representation of the cultural competence of all members of the cultural setting. While explicit knowledge tends to abstraction and fixation of cultural patterns, implicit knowledge must be flexible and can be constantly reformulated.[13]

This distinction is important for three reasons. One, as I have mentioned already, is that any cognitive explication of culture is contested. If explicit abstraction is never complete representation, and if an adequate representation of the cultural competence of all members of a cultural environment in language is impossible, then the question of who represents and whose textual explication becomes dominant is an important one. This is even more relevant if we reflect on intercultural encounters or ecumenical dialogues: with whom in a society do we talk, and who do we encounter?

The second aspect is that a comparison between cultures cannot rely only on the explicit aspects of culture, and cannot be limited to implicit performance of cultural experience. Such comparisons must keep in mind that the problem of translation is

---

[13] Joachim Renn, "Die gemeinsame menschliche Handlungsweise. Das doppelte Übersetzungsproblem des sozialwissenschaftlichen Kulturvergleichs." In: Ilja Srubar, Joachim Renn, Ulrich Wenzel, eds. *Kulturen vergleichen. Sozial- und kulturwissenschaftliche Grundlagen und Kontroversen* (Wiesbaden: Verlag für Sozialwissenschaften, 2005), 195-227, 212.

structurally similar in all cultures since all are shaped by permanent transition from implicit to explicit culture, from performed experience to abstract expression. Although the degrees of abstraction and explicit text creation might differ from one cultural context to another, all cultures share this process of intra-cultural translation.

Common Behaviour

Ludwig Wittgenstein in his *Philosophical Investigations* reflected on this double bind in his famous aphorism in §43: "The meaning of a word is its use in the language game."[14] Meaning is not limited to explicit articulation of culture in linguistic structures or in texts. Neither can cultural meaning be fully represented in the mode of scientific language. Rather, the performative aspects have to be taken into consideration. That is why anthropologist Johannes Fabian argued already 20 years ago for a shift from a hermeneutic and interpretative approach to an ethnological process as a performance in which both the dialogue partners are involved. How, then, is understanding possible? How can we relate to other people's cultural and religious convictions and practices?

In his *Investigations*, Wittgenstein later formulated a possible basis for intercultural encounters. In §206 he states: "The common behaviour of mankind is the system of reference by means of which we interpret an unknown language."[15] This statement is usually interpreted to mean that Wittgenstein is positing the existence of a set (or even a structured system) of human behavioural dispositions, a capacity that human beings share and by which they are distinguished from animals, of being able to master language. The relevance of this thesis for intercultural and inter-religious encounters nevertheless only becomes evident if, as Renn argues, we relate it to the differentiation of pragmatic accessibility from explicit description.[16]

Thus the common behavior of mankind is not to be understood as an anthropological constant or a biological, or at least natural, basis of human action regardless of cultural specifics. Rather, it should be understood as common praxis in a shared situation, a practice that is embedded in culturally different interpretations and may even be distorted by intercultural misunderstanding. The behaviour is not common either in terms of a grounding anthropology or a common explicit religious conviction or the abstract notion that "the religious" is the common point on which understanding should be based.

Instead, the common ground can be found in the shared features of a situation in which each partner acts within the horizon of his or her cultural patterns of

---

[14] Ludwig Wittgenstein, *Philosophische Untersuchungen*, §43 (Frankfurt a.M. 1967), 35.

[15] Wittgenstein, *Philosophische Untersuchungen*, 107.

[16] Renn, *Kulturen vergleichen*, 207.

interpretation. The factual encounter allows for experiences with the culturally other, experiences of success and failure in the interpretation of meaning of the other's cultural performances and the reaction of others to one's own misrepresentation. This can lead step by step to a more practical access to a performative culture as well as to a transformation of one's own respective articulation of a situation.

An Example

All this sounds very abstract. Let me therefore provide one short example. I take it from the field of theology of religions. In this field, the more or less static conceptualization of encounter models as exclusivist, inclusivist and pluralist, as they were first proposed by Allan Race in 1983 and later taken up especially by Perry Schmidt-Leukel, has recently been scrutinized from various sides. Encounters between religions and religious traditions are much more complex and differentiated than this threefold model of a theology of religions can express. Historically, we see that members of different religions do not encounter each other as dogmatic theologians, but first of all as representatives of different cultural environments. Theology is an explicit articulation and a specific interpretation of implicit knowledge.

In a given belief system, to borrow from W.C. Smith, theology is an explicit articulation of faith and in a cultural setting it is an articulation of a lived practice. Theology, therefore, is always contextual. Epistemologically, the contingency of one's own position and the subjectivity of our perception of the world cannot be overcome. The German theologian Reinhold Bernhardt has therefore argued for a "mutual inclusivism" which takes into account "one's own involvement together with a methodological eccentricity."[17] Understanding the other, according to Bernhardt, is never a mere cognitive act, but a careful and fragile attempt in the process of encountering the other to distance oneself from one's own culturally and religiously determined perspective.

As we reflect over the next three days on communication and its theological relevance, I feel we should keep the multiple cultural layers involved in communication processes in mind before we try to formulate theologically-based statements on communication. Or in other words, we should not take for granted that our conviction that communication is a central part of the mission of the Church because it is rooted in the communication of God with this world in Jesus Christ saves us from our constantly misunderstanding each other.

---

[17] Reinhold Bernhardt, *op. cit.*, 233.

The History of Christianity as Media History

Johanna Haberer

Dear colleagues, dear brothers and sisters, our Deputy Dean Bubmann and I welcome you most cordially to our university and faculty. If you have any questions about our university, I will gladly answer them in my capacity as vice-president responsible for teaching, equal opportunities and student support. I also welcome you on behalf of our rector, Professor Grüske, who is always glad when international visitors come to our university.

The Friedrich-Alexander University is one of Germany's leading universities. We have some 26,000 students, of whom approximately 3,000 come from all over the world, and a teaching staff of about 550. We offer a comprehensive range of disciplines forming five faculties covering the Humanities, Law and Economics, Natural Sciences, Engineering and Medicine.

The theology faculty, which is 265 years old this year, was one of the founding faculties of the university. It was named after two electors, Friedrich and Alexander, both of whom were its patrons. But in fact, it was actually a woman, Princess Wilhelmina, the sister of Frederick the Great, who persuaded her husband to found this university.

In the coming days, you will be able to form your own picture of our university and the Theology Department, and I hope that you will have a pleasurable stay. We shall do our utmost to make sure of that!

Communication and mission? How do we communicate our Christian faith and gospel message of justification in a modern media society? What intellectual traditions act as our guide and what communication structures can be developed from them? And what concrete form can the gospel mission take on the basis of the biblical thought patterns in our Jewish/Christian sources in order to pass on what we have inherited, experienced, lived and known?

Before I present a brief examination of the media history of Christianity, I should like, first, to take a look at some concepts.

Medium, Communication, Gospel, Mission

These concepts are changing in theology just as they are changing in other academic disciplines such as media studies, communication and journalism. We are dealing with concepts such as medium, gospel, media, communication and message. Depending on the definitions we decide on, we arrive at completely different results in our debate on the interplay of these concepts.

These considerations are also affected by the ambiguity of these concepts, but it can be assumed that ambiguity may give rise to intellectual productivity! In this lecture, I shall also attempt to pinpoint problems, give pointers, mark out paths, and stimulate creative thinking on gaps in our understanding.

Problematic Concepts

Gospel

First, as an exercise, let us begin with the concept of "gospel." For me as a theologian who thinks journalistically, the word "gospel" means primarily a literary genre, produced by the appearance of Jesus of Nazareth and the salvific (salvatory) meaning of his death, and which was indisputably used for journalistic purposes, that is, to disseminate the portrait of a man whose life was exemplary and open to God, and whose death was mysterious and consistent with his life. The intention of that portrait is to affirm the resurrection and, from a literary point of view, it is open-ended and concludes by presenting human history as open to God and open to the world. From a journalistic point of view, a gospel is a portrait and as a journalistic/literary genre, the narrative presents the consistency of the person with his actions, or the idea that the messenger is at one with his message. Stories of martyrdoms and legends of saints can be regarded as related to this genre of gospel as a portrait in that they too present the portrait of a person.

From a contemporary point of view, it is important that the portrait should essentially reflect the role of the author in our perception of the distinction between what is written and the person who writes, of how the author, on closer inspection, is as self-sacrificial as the person portrayed, and that this genre should reflect a story of relationships. In our theological examination of the concept of "gospel," the particular literary or journalistic genre is subordinate to its contents.

Gospel here means:

- a message of joy for all people, as formulated by Luke (Luke 2);
- good news for the poor (following Isa 61:1, or Matt 11:5);
- Christ's preaching of salvation (Rom 1:1ff or 1 Cor 15:1-4);
- God's saving power for all who believe (Rom 1:16).

Or, in the Reformation's understanding of the gospel, as the certain promise of God's action in reconciling and justifying sinners through the suffering, death and resurrection of Jesus Christ. The concepts of "gospel" and "message" cannot thus be seen as entirely clear-cut.

From a literary-critical point of view, this can, as I have said, mean the appearance of a new and quite unique literary genre which was used for journalistic purposes. However, this also implies the proclamation of a message of salvation without it being made quite clear who its addressees are or who are changed in the course of hearing it. Is it the people, the poor, or the whole of humankind?

Gospel also means speaking of a person, Jesus, of whom it is reported that he uses media in the form of symbolic acts and signs (for example, the money-changers in the temple) in addressing the public, and quite special forms of language such as parables including blessings and admonitions which later developed as literary genres. And, at the same time, the person of Christ is an embodiment of the gospel. Christ is the gospel personified. Christ himself is the medium of the good news, and does not only transmit a message but dishes himself out, distributes and disseminates himself worldwide: "given for you." He acts by himself using media and claims at the same time to be the medium, or intermediary, between God and humankind.

Thus, when we speak of the gospel as a communication medium, we are speaking at one and the same time of a person, of a particular style and manner of using language, of a particular content, and of a journalistic genre.

The media dimension of the gospel in all its nuances is theologically located in "pneumatology," or in the Christian Trinitarian understanding of God. That is the basis of our discourse on Christian belief, and also the mystery of our encounter with God, our understanding, our appropriating that belief for ourselves, and our conviction of its truth and of its transmission to future generations. Our reference to the Holy Spirit thus entails the concept of "gospel" as media and is a reflection of the process of transmission and dissemination, as well as the act of appropriating it and being convinced by it.

So, back to the concept. The words medium, mediating or media call to mind a whole world of associations contained in the concept of communication as well as what is stored in virtual or personal memories, and the persons to whom, it is assumed, communication is addressed. I shall attempt to discuss the whole range of concepts, and examine the pattern of knowledge of the basic media structure and history of the transmission of the Christian faith in the Bible.

The Medium

So, first of all, what is a medium or the media? Our academic study of the media encounters the same problem of definition as with the concept of "gospel" since the words "medium" and "media" are also used with many different shades of meaning. The most comprehensive definition of the concept comes from Marshall McLuhan (1968), who attempted to group under the heading "media" all the devices of civilization that serve to compensate for the deficiencies of the human body. Thus "media" includes, for example, automobiles, clocks, railways or money. Describing it as whatever human beings need to extend their bodily existence frees the concept of "media" from any bounds, and leaves it largely indeterminate.

In the academic study of journalism on the other hand, agreement has been widely reached to understand media in the narrower sense as technical means such as the press, radio, films and television and that "hyper-medium" the internet harnessed to disseminate statements to a potentially limitless public. The concept of "media" is therefore reduced to its overwhelmingly technical aspect. Yet a measure of vagueness remains in that it not only describes the technology but also its products, such as radio and newspapers. Furthermore, "media" also describes the various institutions involved in the production and dissemination of these statements, such as the British Broadcasting Corporation and Associated Press.

If we take this technical concept of the media as our basis, it is not difficult to ascribe a date to the birth of the media and their history. They begin with the invention of printing using moveable type, and continue with the development of many different kinds of media following on from that invention.

Starting with this definition, I shall review the dissemination of the gospel and the Christian message over the past five hundred years and the cultural and ecclesiological consequences of this technological development of the media. The spoken and written precursors of technical media can then simply be regarded as part of the prehistory of the more recent mass communication media.

However, there is no consensus in the academic study of journalism on this understanding of media. The academic study of media which has developed mostly out of the academic study of literature, the humanities and culture, works with a different understanding. Here "media" is applied to any form of communication making use of signs, and the history of the media becomes identical with human history, with cave paintings, body painting, speech and language included in the concept.

If this concept of media is then linked to the concept of communication, our consideration expands to include natural history and any exchange of information in the natural world, even the exchange of information between cells and organisms!

Media expert Werner Faulstich has attempted to divide the concept into different categories in order to go beyond a purely technical concept and to regard it as more than just a phase in human history—this he groups under the heading of media history. He bases his media concept on the worship in primitive societies and their communication centers, which maintained their identity by passing the myths of their origins and their sacrificial rituals on from generation to generation. He thus provides us with a basis for our theological reflection on the media.

Faulstich distinguishes the following stages in the development of the media (cf. Faulstich 1995, 29):

Stage A: The period of primary or human mediation, until c.1500 CE. By human mediation, Faulstich understands communication within small groups such as speech, story-telling, ritual, myth or play and, above all, writing. There is, nevertheless, a question about whether we should regard writing itself, or rather the scrolls, papyrus or letters, as the medium.
Stage B: The change in cultural emphasis to use of a secondary medium—that is, printing. This stage lasts from 1500 to 1900. Print was initially an individual medium that later developed into a means of mass communication. Here, the question arises as to whether book printing accelerated the Reformation or whether the Reformation, with its political, religious and intellectual agenda, actually accelerated the development of the mass media.
Stage C: This stage involves the breakthrough into the tertiary, or electronic, medium.
Stage D: Since the end of the 20th century, this stage, according to Faulstich, has involved the development of the quaternary, or digital, medium, allowing the media to be used interactively and by individuals.

Faulstich, like the German studies and media expert Jochen Hörisch, also approaches the theme of the media from the history of culture. They both see in human history a very close interaction between religion and the media. Hörisch, taking up McLuhan, defines the media as "interactive coordinators" (2001, 65), as tools which enable the improbable—such as a moon landing—to appear to us as probable. He describes media history, beginning with this definition, as the history of three mass means of communication: the Eucharist as the first; money as the second; and the internet as the third. This is also a theoretical approach to the media that can fit into a theological framework that regards religion, including the Christian religion, as a manifestation of humankind's attempt to find meaning and basic coherence, an attempt that is reflected in cultural phenomena. Based on that approach, Wilhelm Gräb, who teaches Practical Theology at the Free University of Berlin, postulates "theology as media hermeneutics" and "religious history as media history." He describes the task of theology in the world of the media as "the ability to interpret meaning." If we thus proceed beyond the purely technical definition of the media, there opens up before us a creative field of speculation in which theology and media science can academically cooperate.

Biblical Patterns of Knowledge

How is communication through media spelt out in the Old and New Testaments?

Let us examine first some Old Testament texts to see how direct intervention by God develops into an indirect transmission of tradition. That can be seen from the narrative of the setting down of the Torah in written form.

With the giving of the Ten Commandments as the basis of God's covenant with God's people, a written text becomes the center of the religious relationship because of the direct and intimate nature of the encounter, which is described as being of the utmost importance for the people and is thus made public. In the presence of a written document, the tables of the law, so the story goes, Jahweh's attentiveness and presence is assured. In Nehemiah 8, we hear of a book being read aloud and expounded: "Ezra opened the book. All the people could see him… and as he opened it, all stood up. [The Levites] read from the Book of the law of God, making it clear and giving the meaning so that the people could understand what was being read" (Neh 8: 5-8). Here we can observe a development—following the path laid down by Faulstich—documenting how worship fell into the background in favor of written tradition. The reality of God's presence loses its personal immediacy and is entrusted to a book, a medium in which memory is stored, the interpretation of which requires particular abilities. Thus a new knowledge elite, new traditions of interpretation and places for interpretation emerge, and then comes censorship. Censorship comes into being at the moment when it becomes possible to store signs and texts, preserve them in archive form and thus to generate historical relevance out of the memory of past generations detached from contemporary persons and their times.

In addition to the book of Ezra, the Old Testament prophetic tradition makes reference, for example in Jeremiah 36, to writing down communications from God and making them public. We see here Yahweh's direct message of doom to Jeremiah for Israel's salvation, and that message is linked with the order to write it down: "Take a scroll and write on it all the words I have spoken to you concerning Israel, Judah and all the other nations from the time I began speaking to you in the reign of Josiah till now" (Jer 36:2). Jeremiah takes a scroll and dictates the words that had been revealed to him to a scribe. He directs his scribe to go to the temple and there read out from the scroll in order to call the people to repentance in order to save them from disaster. A government informer learns of this activity, reports it, and Baruch (the scribe) together with his scroll is summoned by the leaders. When they hear its words, they are frightened because of their political relevance and decide to read them to the king. Jeremiah and his scribe are told to go and hide.

The scroll is then read to the king, and he reacts by destroying it. He throws it into the fire—an early example of book-burning. With the birth of a medium that stores memory, censorship also begins. Prophets and journalists exercise professions related to such a medium in that they make social comment, convey God's commands, describe social conditions, legal and political power relationships. With this possibility of recording and preserving memories independently of individuals, the writing of history and historical comment according to the standards of God's promise and command also emerges. The interpretation of history in a prophetic sense as well as the development of a prophetic approach to the action of God in the history of God's people are thus dependent on having a medium that stores it.

In Jeremiah, we can also see the immediacy of the message and how it is mediated by being passed on. The prophet receives the message in "total awareness."[1] He hears it, responds and deals with it, sometimes offering resistance and sometimes in sorrow but always as an individual. There is no ecstatic union of the messenger with the message in the sense of the prophet's individuality being eliminated. There is no preparatory ritual, no meditation. However, as human mediator or medium (as Faulstich puts it), the messenger bears responsibility for the message, accepts even physical suffering and suffers in and with the message. In order to communicate it publicly, he uses public speeches and symbolic acts—devices that can be regarded as media. The prophet is not only a commentator on politics, participating in the opposition, but he is at the same time a factor in politics. The prophet is hugely significant for the memory and transmission of national traditions and historical political knowledge, and an essential educator (cf. Hardmeier 1990).

In 1889, the French orientalist Ernest Renan described the work of the prophet from a journalistic perspective: "The eighth-century prophet is a journalist, working at large, who incorporates in his own person what he is reporting, accompanying it with mime and gesture, and indeed often translating it into symbolic acts. The aim above all is to impress the people and attract a crowd. To achieve that, the prophet did not shrink from the sort of outrageous behavior so beloved of modern journalism. He stands at a place where many people pass by, particularly at the city gate. To attract hearers, he uses the most ingenious advertising techniques, feigns madness, uses new words and unfamiliar expressions, and himself carries around written placards. When his hearers have gathered, he hits out at them with hard words, threatens and influences his public, at one point with kindly words, and then with savage mockery. And so the image of the popular preacher is created" (quoted by Faulstich 1997, 185).

The direct relationship of the prophet with Jahweh is, of course, a literary device. We are told of the prophet's immediate relation with God, but this is impressively related in narrative and dramatic form—as it were, journalisti-

---

[1] Hans Walter Wolff, *Studien zur Prophetie – Probleme und Erträge* (München: Theologische Bücherei 76, 1987), 33.

cally—so that the literary device evokes an immediate spiritual bond with the recipient and thus predisposes hearers to absorb the message.

The story of Jeremiah ends with the glorious victory of the published word over the king's censorship. In the last verse we read, "So Jeremiah took another scroll and gave it to the scribe Baruch... and, as Jeremiah dictated, Baruch wrote on it all the words of the scroll that Jehoiakim king of Judah had burned in the fire" (Jer 36:32). The message described as coming directly from God is, in the literary narrative, given historical power by being put down in writing and published by the prophet. Using journalistic ideas, we can say that relevance, which feeds on news value, is preserved by being published through:

- the literary convention of the prophet's direct relationship with God as an indication of his legitimacy and authority, in short his divine commission;
- the content of the message, at once threatening existence but also conveying salvation;
- the personal testimony given by the prophet;
- the critical situation in which the communication takes place;
- and ultimately, the public status and value of what is said, recorded in written form and then, as an act of resistance to authority, again recorded for public reading as theological comment on contemporary history.

Human Beings as the Medium

The prophetic tradition also tells of symbolic births (cf. Jer 8). A child is born and is given a name that contains the message in a nutshell. It is the concept of an act of procreation that produces a message. That can also be further developed in relation to the story of Jesus.

Jesus left no writings behind him. Quite unlike Mohammed later, he dictated nothing. Neither did he receive messages. Instead, according to the literary device of the gospels that we do have, he declared himself to be God's message and also God's image in the world. The reaction is described as a mixture of denial, hatred, wonder, amazement and belief. His declaration strikes everyone differently and triggers off fresh discussion. The putting into writing of Jesus' words, speeches and sermons, the creation of a new and never-repeated literary genre with considerable public effectiveness, was accompanied by a further literary media genre of reflection and discourse: the epistle, or letter. It is Paul's achievement that has left an effective historical mark on Christianity's disciples and students of Scripture.

Paul's epistles were public documents intended to be read aloud in public to guide a recently founded community and as a basis for further discussion. An epistle is a stimulus to engage in discussion, a media form that creates direct encounter between those engaged in discussion. An epistle seeks a response, takes those to whom it is addressed seriously, stimulates reflection. Through repeated public readings, argument and controversy, through weighing it up and comparing it, through addressing the reader and eliciting a reaction and a response, the epistle enables people to appropriate its message for themselves.

The basic Christian medium, the man Jesus and his message, are reflected in the journalistic genres they use: the symbol of the Eucharist, the gospel as a literary construct, the letter as a means to enable its readers and audiences participatively to appropriate it. We see the power of literary aesthetics, the nature of the discourse of the journalistic genre, public availability as a criterion for transmission, exposition as part of this appropriation. The media communication of the message in Christianity provides the stage for direct encounter.

Incidentally, it seems to me that the Corinthians were already discussing the distinction between the person and the medium when they said of Paul, "His letters are weighty and forceful, but in person he is unimpressive and his speaking amounts to nothing" (2 Cor 10:10). There are thus different gifts: charisms involved in direct encounter and charisms involved in transmitting the message.

From this review of the various media patterns used to communicate the divine message of salvation, I should like to draw the following conclusions.

Some Theses

The biblical tradition indicates that Jewish/Christian culture is a media culture in which religion makes use of a great variety of media. Jewish/Christian religion very early on came to regard written texts as being of great historical relevance. For our contemporary communication task, that means storing developments in belief and in church life in our memory, and considering them of great importance in contemporary debate and decision-making.

The public transmission of a word from God received by individuals (messages of healing, messages of woe, messages of salvation) is part of the task. That means that Christianity has never been a secret society. Public communication is essential to Christianity. Media communication, from the scroll to the internet, is an important factor in maintaining public standards. That applies particularly in the prophetic tradition, in which the memory and transmission of what has been said makes it possible to produce a critical approach to history. In the multi-faceted media portrait of the person of Jesus, the human medium and the genre concept are combined and each has a journalistic dimension in its own distinctive way.

Gospel as person, content and genre is an essential element in an open conversation, which can result in either acceptance or rejection. We are never dealing with unquestioned acceptance of what is heard, seen or read, but with the appropriation for oneself of individual acts or processes. This implies that the organization and conduct of Protestant journalism must include the possibility for a free exchange of opinions, for criticism, and also a certain detachment from secular and ecclesiastical institutions.

Protestant media work enables people to make contact with the Christian message, enables discussion to take place as to its truth, and enables people to learn as they discuss.

Protestant media work provides information on the nature and gift of faith; it provides a forum for different understandings of the faith and guidance within the church; and it is charged with performing the duty of chronicler for the institution, and maintaining dialogue between church institutions and parish members. It also reports on the diaconal work of the church in society.

It is thus highly advisable that the public work of the church and Protestant journalism be institutionally separate, for Christian journalism must be independent, under obligation only to the freedom of the gospel. Christian journalism is a vehicle of freedom and, in a time when societies are divided into lobbying groups, it provides a remnant of independent communication, detached from institutions, which is what is implied in the heritage of the Reformation churches.

Bibliography

Faulstich, Werner. *Grundwissen Medien, zweite Auflage.* München: Fink, 1995.

Faulstich, Werner. *Das Medium als Kult. Von den Anfängen bis zur Spätantike (8. Jahrhundert).* Göttingen: Vandenhoeck und Ruprecht, 1997.

Hardmeier, Christof. *Prophetie im Streit vor dem Untergang Judas.* Berlin, New York: de Gruyter, 1990.

Helmke, Julia. Kirche, Film und Festivals. Geschichte sowie Bewertungskriterien evangelischer und ökumenischer Juryarbeit in den Jahren 1948 bis 1988. In *Studien zur Christlichen Publizistik*, Bd. XI. Erlangen, 2005.

Hörisch, Jochen. *Der Sinn und die Sinne. Eine Geschichte der Medien.* Frankfurt am Main: Eichborn Verlag, 2001.

McLuhan, Marshall. *Die magischen Kanäle.* Düsseldorf, Wien: Econ-Verlag, 1968.

Wolff, Hans Walter. *Studien zur Prophetie – Probleme und Erträge.* München: Theologische Bücherei 76, 1987.

Africa

Communication in Mission and the "New Culture" – The African Challenges

Brenda Akpan

Introduction

It is a known fact that the ministry of the church inevitably implies communication, be it mission, Christian nurture, development, worship, education or service. Such practice of communication when carried out effectively helps provide a human definition of communication as the "sharing of experiences" or "the transfer of meaning" or "the transmission of values."[1]

While it is not proper to limit communication to these factors due to its ascribed content and relationship perspectives, communication remains the human cement that glues our society and cultures together. It serves as an emotional and intellectual connecting rod between individuals, groups and institutions, thereby becoming the cultural imperative that allows societies to exist and flourish.

How these features play out in different parts of the world depends on various factors since the church does not operate in isolation from society and "the Church cannot wall itself up in a cultural ghetto at a time when humanity as a whole is passing into the electronic age."[2] Mission in Africa in the face of the "new culture" in communication will be discussed here within that global framework, where politics, hunger, poverty, violence, lack of social welfare, health facilities and security etc. impact and influence what communication should be and how it functions, especially in view of the realities on the African continent, where religious conflicts and other failures of co-existence have become a great challenge.

---

[1] B. Akpan, "Communication in Africa: The Nigerian Perspective." A paper presented at a meeting of ALCINET at the LWF Consultation on Poverty in Arusha, Tanzania, in July 2005.

[2] A. Dulles, "The Church Is Communications." *Catholic Mind*, Vol. 69, 1971.

Theological Reflections

As Shorter once observed:

> ... human beings are deeply tied to culture and cannot be evangelized unless
> they are addressed in terms of their culture. The Gospel itself cannot be known
> except through the medium of culture.[3]

Communication theology postulates reveal that "religion is all about communication between God and humanity and among peoples themselves."
Available records show that in every era, different religions have used the best
communication media and strategies to propagate their teachings and ideologies.
Religious meanings have been made, preserved and transmitted through oral,
written and printed texts, symbolizations such as rituals, art, icons and even
architecture. Above all, messages were and are being passed on through many
forms of theological reflection. Thus "communicating the word of God is the
central mission of the church and hence, a more communicative church means
a more missionary and pastoral church. All her ministries are intended to make
this communication effective... and at the service of all other ministries."[4]

One of the ways by which the mission of the church is accomplished is through
evangelization. To evangelize means to promote the communion of people through
the proclamation of values of the kingdom. According to St John, God's revelation
is the "word of life," "the eternal life... made visible to us" in Jesus Christ, and the
proclamation of this good news is intended to engage everyone in fellowship with
one another and with the Trinity so that all may have the fullness of life. (1 John
1:1-4) This proves that the explicit goal of God's self-communication is to give life:
"I have come so you may have life and have it abundantly." (John 10:10)

Since the essence of mission is to communicate life, this calls for a comprehensive perspective on mission and ministry whose focus transcends religious
and spiritual boundaries to include the holistic liberation of every human being
and the entire universe itself into the freedom of the children of God, who are
created in the image and likeness of God, who is communication and communion. (Eilers, 2004) Eilers' perspective extends the view of communication
beyond the modern mass media to all the ways and means of communicating
in human society with special bearing on mission. This includes traditional

---

[3] A. Shorter, *Toward a Theology of Inculturation* (New York: Orbis Books 1988), 27.

[4] J. Palakeel, *Exploring Guidelines for the Communications Ministry*, 2006 (**www.mstworld.org/
subpages/DC/Guidelines.pdf**), downloaded 1.2.2009.

and cultural means of communication, referred to as social communications and defined by Eilers (1994) as "sharing meaning through signs."

The general current view of communication mainly through technology is therefore inspired by the conviction that "the media of social communication can and should be instruments in the church's program of re-evangelization and new evangelization in the contemporary world." Because they are means devised under God's providence, the church could feel guilty before the Lord if it did not utilize these powerful means. Therefore "Communication can be said to be at the core of the Christian understanding of God, man and the world." (Ferguson, 2005)

The apostolic mandate for mission found in the Gospel of Matthew (28:18-20) challenges all Christians to share the good news of Jesus with others both in their own "homes" and beyond their geographical boundaries.

The Acts of the Apostles tells the beginning of that mission story. The scene is set with the ascension of Jesus, and the beginning of the new era of ecclesia. In Acts, ecclesia refers to a community of God's people, men and women living with concrete hopes, undeniable anxieties, and most of all, a willingness to be changed by God, and to bring change to their communities. In Acts, people share their learning, their belongings, and their personal experiences of the good news. Their very actions define mission as the sharing of the good news both in proclamation of God's word (communicating) as well as in material welfare. This act of sharing has no boundaries.

Kanyoro[5] describes the entire biblical drama of the Pentecost event: the apostles and disciples were gathered in prayer (Acts 1:2-14) when suddenly those present heard the sound of a mighty wind rush upon them. This sound filled the whole house in which they were sitting (Acts 2:2). They saw tongues of fire issuing forth and resting on each one of them. They all acted—by speaking words of prophecy in many languages. Each one heard the other as if he or she were speaking the same language.

According to Kanyoro, "the real point of the outpouring of the Holy Spirit was to make the connection, the bridge, between Jesus and the believers, and to remove the barriers that separated the believers in terms of age, gender and class. The outpouring of the Spirit is a very conspicuous event—with visible and physical signs, recognized by all—apostles, menservants, maidservants, the youth, the old, the Jews and the Gentiles. What other affirmation would be needed as evidence that, in the new order, we all have value in God's eyes?"[6]

---

[5] M. Kanyoro, "Thinking Mission in Africa." *IRM*, Vol. LXXXVII no. 345, April 1998.

[6] *Op. cit.*

The point being made here can be viewed in many ways. It conveys the message that the outpouring of the Holy Spirit not only conferred the status of "communicator" on all believers (those charged with the duty of accepting and maintaining the connection and bridge already created by the outpouring), but also charged to perform such a task without any barriers.

The various areas of discussion here are addressed to support the fact that it is difficult realistically to discuss mission and ministry in today's world without relating it to the communication revolution of our times and its cultural implications. "The church on earth is by its very nature missionary." This is drawn from the "fountain-like love" of God the Father and the Holy Trinity. Avery Dulles told the bishops in America in 1971 that the church by her very essence, calling and nature is communication. She exists to communicate and, thus, "church is communication."[7] He states:

> … the very life and function of the missionary church is to communicate the Trinitarian love to people. The Trinitarian communicating God also reveals himself in communicating with his creatures. He uses all ways and means of human communication, he communicates verbally and non-verbally. He communicates with signs and actions. Jesus Christ communicates through the whole way of his life. The entire Old Testament is a document of God's communication with his people. (Harvey, 2006)

The essence of mission is to communicate life. The word mission means "sending," and this makes mission and communication identical in a way. Thus, mission is communication. It is the communication and sharing of faith with others, especially those not yet reached. In this understanding, communication is not something for specialists alone but a dimension for every Christian as a member of the church, to be reflected in daily life. (Harvey, 2006) It means also that our communication trainings should be organized not just as media training sessions for specialists but an essential element of our faith. The Acts of the Apostles remind us of the fact that every one of the early Christians communicated his or her faith. A major area of challenge for mission activity is in the sharing of faith experiences on the circumstances of life. This "sending" process, which started with the Pentecost under the promise and power of the Holy Spirit, "is the driving force for communication and mission through the centuries."[8]

---

[7] A. Dulles, *op. cit.*

[8] Kanyoro, *op. cit.*

African Challenges in Mission

Various researchers have noted that the idea of mission and missionaries has many complex connotations for Christians in Africa. It usually evokes images of white brothers and sisters who come from foreign countries, often with money, to serve in remote rural settings and help run churches in various capacities. Such researchers have also noted that the Christian understanding of mission often equates it with "receiving" rather than "giving" something. "We feel that mission can only take place when one has to travel to foreign lands and witness to people other than one's own. Thus mission was never thought of as something that can be done by us for our people. We never saw ourselves as having the rights and responsibilities as missionaries of God's work."[9]

Africa is a continent of many uncertainties and woes. "Catastrophes, natural and man-made disasters, epidemics, political upheavals, wars and unending economic and social disorders, to mention but a few, render the continent unsafe for even the indigenes. The lack and sometimes total absence of hope of future redress is in itself a big human burden." Today, we have the extra burden of the deadly HIV/AIDS virus. The economic situation of our countries does not allow for even the essential basic needs of the majority of their populations to be met. Whatever the political or military dispensation, the state only continues to inherit an ever-greater national debt, while the accumulation of national wealth by a few knows no bounds. The frequent threats and deaths from female circumcision, vesicovaginal fistulas (VVF), have not been taken up as an issue by the church in order to teach something new about culture and human dignity. African women are "being silenced daily by maternal mortality, cultural prescriptions, illiteracy and endless daily chores that make them grow old before their time." As we consider these sorrowful situations, the question is: "What does the Holy Spirit give us, Christians in Africa, by way of power and ability, to do in our setting and time?"[10]

Facing our Mission Challenges

Perhaps when we look at our troubled Africa, imprisoned by wars, debt, famine, corruption, political irresponsibility, held to ransom by disease and poverty, blinded by elitism, tribalism, materialism, illiteracy—the list seems endless—we likewise see

---

[9] A. Shorter, *Religious Obedience in Africa* (Nairobi: Paulines Publications Africa, 2000).

[10] Kanyoro, *op. cit.*

almost no beginning or end to what our mission could be.[11] Therefore, we wonder how individual Christians and the churches in Africa can or should witness to the risen Jesus within this situation in which so much effort is needed just to alleviate human suffering and improve community life. Incidents in the recent past, including civil wars in particular, have left Africans unable to prevent the atrocities inflicted upon human life. How can we, as a church, be involved in programs which provide not only for the witness of the gospel by word, but also by deed? Is our task only to preach the gospel but neglect the wellbeing of followers? Or is it not, rather, part of our mission as the church in Africa to respond to the socio-economic needs of our communities, and to the daily violations of human rights? (Ekanem, 2008)

The Book of Acts offers many links to the challenges facing us as Africans today and forces us to reflect again on the passage on Pentecost as it relates to our continent… and indeed to many other parts of the world where the plurality of languages creates difficulties of communication across boundaries, poor governance, ethnic conflicts, illiteracy and many other barriers.

Kanyoro places responsibility for most of Africa's woes on the doorsteps of leadership both in society and the church:

> We on the continent of Africa must reflect on the question of accountability for our actions, both past and present, otherwise we are not going to be able to leave any heritage for the future of our continent. One of our most urgent tasks is to remember the future. Do we care enough for our continent? […] many of us will say that we are already involved in many good deeds. Some of the churches are growing, we have translated the Bible into many languages, we have equipped churches and seminaries with modern technological gadgets. We have established seminaries, radio and printing outfits. We have schools and hospitals. We have gathered in the street children, fed the hungry, visited the lonely, given refuge to victims of war and other displaced people; we have tended the sick and dying. We have been busy binding wounds, but have not stopped the war. We have prepared bodies for burial, but have not stopped the killing.[12]

Ekanem (2008) confirms that being in mission in Africa should go beyond good deeds, and questions the level of involvement and efficiency of churches in the actual mission work and witnessing on the continent. How many members of the growing churches are real Christians?

---

[11] E. Ekanem, "Commununication and Mission in Nigeria." Presented at the opening of the ALCINET workshop, Calabar, Nigeria. July 2008.

[12] Kanyoro, *op. cit.*

The "New Culture" of Communication as Mission Challenge

In the period from 800 to 1700 CE, the church was the leader in technological advancement for theological reasons. (Noble, 1997) Ferguson (2005) confirms that "Religion has traditionally been one of the first elements of society to embrace technological advances, from moveable type to radio to online ordinations through the internet." What do we mean by "new culture" and what does it look like?

In many parts of the world including Africa, it is not unusual to see a peasant farmer in the fields or a fisherman in his canoe doing his work, and at the same time talking on his cell phone. Within the last decade, cell phones, apart from computers and other technology, have found their way into every corner of the globe regardless of culture, status and class, and have become a part of life for many, especially in the developing world.

The pervasiveness of technology is perhaps most observable in the proliferation of these cell phones, with some advanced models enabling users to access the internet, watch TV, listen to music, take photos, send and receive e-mail and text messages and do many more things which were never part of life in Africa. Their advent has implanted a new culture in the area of communication.

While the global diffusion of this technology into every nook and cranny has much power for good, it also has its downside. Some users feel trapped in the electronic web while others become technology addicts. Addiction, distraction, interruption are perhaps the most recognized problems associated with popular communications and media technology.

Within the religious realm, an emerging view of communication known as the inculturation perspective is inspired by the missiological theory of evangelization of cultures. What it preaches is that "It is not enough to use the media simply to spread the Christian message and the church's authentic teaching since the evangelization of modern culture depends to a great extent on the influence of the media. It is also necessary to integrate that message into the new culture created by modern communications."[13]

Many researchers (Traber, 1989; Webb, 1989; Palakeel, 2000) have stressed the deeper reality involved in this view since the "new culture" originates not just from whatever content is eventually expressed, but from the fact that there are new ways of communicating, with new languages, new techniques and new psychology. They contend that these new ways are no longer just skills and training for the use of the media or simply the use of these modern media, but that they call for a shift in thinking and approach. This new perspective brings into focus the fact that

---

[13] Palakeel, *op. cit.*

Christian communication must start from and be embedded in the life of people and reflected in their cultures, which is an important element in mission studies.

The biggest challenge facing communication theology is to transcend the instrumental and inculturation perspective to an integration approach, where communication is valued as an integral element of evangelizing and pastoral ministry. Where also, as Palakeel puts it, "Communication is considered as the defining factor in the creation of culture and construction of meanings, rather than a mere instrument of interaction." He draws our attention to the fact that the digital revolution we are witnessing is not just technological progress or a change in medium:

> It has affected the way people think, feel, behave, and live, and even up to the mental habits of knowing and making sense/meaning. To be an effective evangelizer today, the church has to go beyond an instrumental view of communication and embrace the new style, language and culture of communication at every time and place.[14]

Eilers (2002) referring to the *Redemptoris Missio,* an encyclical letter on "Mission ad Gentes," offers a few considerations to further clarify these points.[15]

According to him, the "new culture" and reality of modern communication is more "determined by emotions than rationality." Most broadcast and print media are less institutionalized and aim at the emotional needs and expectations of the public rather than their rational minds. TV and radio programs lack depth and do not cater either to families or to constructive reasoning. "Reality shows" like "Big Brother" that are shown in many countries around the world are a good example. The growing number of movies with implicit and explicit sexual content is also a case in point. Some countries now have to censor movies in order to protect society from decay. Even the selection and presentation of news is increasingly determined by emotion rather than facts. Images, music and words build and aim more at emotions than thinking. Communicators believe that if people's emotions are stimulated and satisfied, their ratings will rise because the viewers/listeners feel fulfilled.

In Africa, these issues are very evident. The Nigerian film industry, Nollywood, for example, has thrived on its appeal to the Nigerian psyche (young and old). Its lighthearted nature and realism makes it appeal to those who are bored and frustrated. "But is the content morally okay? Are we teaching the right things when we show youths in every film how to take over other peoples'

---

[14] Palakeel, *op. cit.*

[15] Pope John Paul II, *Redemptoris Missio. On the Permanent Validity of the Church's Missionary Mandate.* Papal Encyclical, December 1990.

husbands by soliciting the help of native doctors? People are no longer in a position to decipher what is right or wrong in the society."[16]

Church religious services are no longer periods of decorum and communication with the Holy Spirit. Pastors on my continent now use worship periods for theatrical performances, imitating their counterparts in the West by jumping around the stage and distracting their congregations, with little or no lesson in their messages. They want to blow a breath and have the whole congregation falling down as if a miracle had been performed. (Nketiah,1958) This new culture in communication has overwhelmed the continent.

Anthony Rogers reports that under the heading of "new communication," we find information overload, a lack of vision and of a sense of social responsibility, and a highly organized system of misinformation and image management which Christian communicators are supposed to accept as another "mission" area of our time. There is a gradual eclipse of truth, of the notion of justice and peace.

These trends point to the fact that we as Christians lack the "moral authority" to clarify the difference between right and wrong as far as communication is concerned. Lacking vision and a clear view of reality, religions themselves are too much preoccupied with their internal interests and concerns—a fact which questions the very mission of the church.[17]

Globalized effect

In the "new culture" the "world of modern communications has no borders." Happenings and "cultural products" from all over the world are accessible to everybody in a globalized media world. As mentioned earlier in this paper, the shores of Africa have not escaped the enormous new possibilities provided by satellite technology. The flow of news in one direction (from North to South) makes it the more challenging. Africans in Africa read and receive news about the continent from the foreign press, from CNN etc., and of course it is mostly the negative news. In fact, African news gets to the Western media where it is censored and sent back to Africa.

> Whenever I am outside my continent, I am starved of constructive news from Africa except of course when there is some war, a coup d'état or the assassination of a president of a country etc. Even humanitarian and development stories are given a negative slant, e.g., refugees pictured must be babies with runny noses hanging on to the dry drooping breasts of their mothers rather than those who have been cleaned up and fed

---

[16] B. Akpan, "Youth Perspectives in the Nigerian Film Industry." A paper presented at a conference of Nigerian women journalists, Abuja, Nigeria, June 2002.

[17] A. Rogers, "Fighting Poverty: Politics and Policies." Paper delivered at the Signus Asia conference, Kuala Lumpur, Malaysia, October 2004.

for the day in the tents—nothing constructive. The tribesmen of Africa are generally referred to on the streets of the West as barbaric, heathen, backward etc.[18]

In many ways, we in Africa have deserved this sort of evaluation because "the media in Africa plays down the voices of women and poor [people]; deceit and corruption by politicians give a false notion that in a democracy the majority is always right" with scarcely any regard for universal ethical norms.[19]

Youth

Satellite TV has projected the "new culture" in communication into the remotest parts of the African continent, wherever some form of electricity can be generated. As a result, communication in mission in Africa is facing many challenges, especially with young people. A major threat is the upsurge of Pentecostalism. Influenced by what they see about Pentecostalism on satellite TV from the West, young people consider this as the "in thing." So they now find the orthodox churches boring, their liturgy monotonous and their hymns dull. They want to be like Westerners even if they can't go there. They want to wear whatever they wish when they go to church; young women no longer want to tie their hair back; they prefer to wear trousers, jeans and short blouses and keep their hair untied. While the Pentecostals accept this, such behavior is against our culture as Africans.

The Gospel

Church worship services in Africa have always interspersed the gospel messages with familiar local songs backed by traditional drumming and dancing. Today, these have been mostly replaced by foreign music. It is difficult at an interdenominational service to recognize song lyrics and tunes and participate in the fellowship. What we hear now is foreign gospel music in various musical styles, backed up by electronic gadgets, with lyrics on a screen rather than in print. (Beach, 2005) This situation has taken away a primary anchor of worship, that is, corporate singing. As Harvey (2006) asks, "Where is the freedom to repeat a verse or chorus on the spur of the moment under the leading of the spirit? Where is the opportunity to follow the spirit's spontaneous inspiration and insert an unplanned song? Can the careful scripting of a worship service in a wired world allow enough room for the spirit to break in and do something unprogrammed?" (Sample, 1998) Harvey questions whether technology has

---

[18] Akpan, *op. cit.*

[19] Ekanem, *op. cit.*

not robbed us of the mystical moments of worship that Heidegger[20] called "poetizing in the realm of Nature."

The "new culture" that shows well-dressed sophisticated pastors on stage in glassy church buildings causes problems when African church leaders and pastors want to wear silk suits and drive Porsche cars like those they watch on TV while in fact their salaries can hardly sustain them and their families, their church buildings are still made with mud blocks and their only hope is a foreign partner somewhere. They therefore resort to squeezing funds out of poor members, using passages in the Bible to buttress their claims. A popular one is "Give and it shall be given unto you," or "The Lord loves a cheerful giver." They also want to be guarded by security operatives and remain aloof from the flock whose welfare and interest they are expected to protect. It is common to find church leaders aligning with rich church members even if they are known in the community to be criminals and traditional religion worshippers.

Morality

In the past, young people grew up in societies based on stable, cultural, moral and spiritual traditions. In Africa, a young person greets the older one first, and communication starts from there. An older child picks food first before younger ones, and respect for each other is maintained. In former times, an adult could accost a child loitering in the street during school hours and even administer punishment there and then to ensure a future for the community. A bishop dared not talk love to a church member. All these traditions are waning fast under the onslaught of other models transmitted by the "new culture," when young people, for instance, see on TV their peers in the Western world talking back to their parents. An African girl in Europe or America now sees an elderly African lady and calls her by her first name. If it is part of our missionary activity and calling to defend culture and people's dignity, then what does this mean for the preservation of local cultures, and especially for the young people in these areas? This is food for thought for all of us.

The "new culture" lives on "new rituals" which challenge the impact of traditional and especially religious rituals. Eilers quoted Gregory Goethals' reflection on this phenomenon and called it the "Golden Calf" when he wrote about the "TV Ritual: Worship on the Video-Altar." The opening and closing of the Olympic Games, sports events in general, but also national mourning at the death of presidents (and Lady Diana) are some rituals we can mention

---

[20] Quoted in S. Harvey, "Caputo on Heidegger and Ethics." Master thesis, McGill University, Montreal, Canada, 2002.

along with our own personal "ritual" submission to certain media programs. These rituals have come to be accepted as substitutes to those of religious life. Carey sees rituals as acts that help to maintain culture and society.

> They are associated with performance rather than movements, participation rather than consumption, meaning or beauty rather than strategy and results, evocation or calling rather than influence or effectiveness. A ritual is not something one is mere audience to but rather something where one is participant in.[21]

Such ritual communication is concerned about the communicative ways and means which maintain the fiber of society, to share, participate, associate, create fellowship and enjoy common faith and convictions. Religion is one aspect of life that provided for such experiences in an unimaginable number of ways. This seems to have been taken over by the modern means of communication which determine and dominate the life of people more than any religious commitment. The shared interest of people in religious rituals and experiences is gradually waning and giving way to secular rituals which substitute for religion. Examples are secularized weddings, burials and entertainment which are ritualized in many ways. African Christians no longer mourn the dead properly. The younger generation with Western education are treating our "dead" carelessly. This is against our cultural values.

Modern communication culture is "entertainment-oriented," largely in response to the stresses and strains of life in Africa. It has now come to the point where viewers of TV news or films and readers of newspapers and periodicals do not seek knowledge but just want to kill time by being entertained by sensational stories and light-hearted reports on stars, politicians, housekeeping, new cooking recipes, etc. They prefer information presented in an entertaining way that requires no effort to try to forge understanding. Today's audiences surrender to programs that feed their curiosity and entertainment needs. Rather than listen to serious broadcasts relating to their own communities, some of which could save their lives, not to mention religious discussion groups, people rush to watch stars perform.

The world of social communication is strongly determined by commercial considerations. Africa has joined the Western media where public service broadcasting has been taken over by private commercial radio and TV stations. The downturn in the world economy has forced communication undertakings the world over to generate funds to sustain themselves and the establishment. Entertainment programs and news are produced according to ratings, the personality concerned and how much money is paid. Consumerism is promoted

---

[21] J. Carey, *Communication as Culture. Essays on Media and Society*. (New York/London: Routledge, 1992).

through aggressive advertising, most of which fills up peak air time, and the values presented in these programs and advertising are no longer the values of Christian life. This is the same scenario in Africa. Most if not all media outfits are commercialized in order to break even. Getting news on air costs a lot of money. It becomes worse when the customer is a church organization perceived to be generating regular funds. So the bigger and more famous a church is, the more money is charged. This financial perspective has killed evangelism through the media for many churches, especially those in the Lutheran communion in the developing world where there is a lack of funds.

William Fore in his book on "the shaping of faith values and culture" sees the values promoted in the modern communication world this way:

> Power heads the list: power over others; power over nature… close to power are the values of wealth and property, the idea that everything can be purchased and that consumption is an intrinsic good. The values of narcissism, of immediate gratification of wants and comfort follow close behind. Thus the mass media world tells us that we are basically good, that happiness is the chief end of life, and that happiness consists in obtaining material goods. The media transform the value of sexuality into sex appeal, the value of self respect into pride, the value of the will-to-live into the will-to-power. They exacerbate acquisitiveness into greed; they deal with insecurity by generating more insecurity and anxiety by generating more anxiety. They change the value of recreation into competition and the value of rest into escape. And perhaps worst of all, the media constrict our experience and substitute the media world for the real world so that we become less and less able to make the fine value-judgments that living in such a complex world requires. (Fore, 1987)

Ineke de Fijter (2004) notes that advertising very often builds and enforces such media culture where religious symbols and rituals are also used for selling and commercial purposes. For example, a clothing chain in the Netherlands calls itself G-sus, using symbols and religious language like "G-sus comes" and G-sus "saves." Unilever, another Dutch food company, promoted seven new ice-creams with the names of the seven capital sins, a Belgian beer company related its beer to "the eleventh commandment: thou shall enjoy," a cheese spread was advertised by angels….

In Africa, using religious symbols as an advert would spark off a serious religious conflict. These are serious matters in the African religious context.

The ICT

The new information and communication technologies (ICT) bring an additional dimension into the "new culture" by opening new challenges for a missionary approach to communication. The absence of interactivity which follows the "Religion Online" project is a good example. The ICT project is growing in many countries of the world and so are the many people, especially young people, who try to express and live "online religion." Eilers (2004) challenges how virtual reality can change people, answer their deeper needs and give them an opportunity to express their religious desires, and calls for serious study and research on the missionary and evangelical dimension beyond talking about "e-vangelism" and "cyber-missionaries." He stresses the need for the various dimensions of the "new culture" to be considered as "mission" fields and emphasizes that "We cannot deny that we live in a growing total communication culture and our mission fields are not any more geographically determined but rather by these new challenges."

However, in Africa where one can only manage to access the web a few times a month due to lack of funds and electricity, these can be termed as future discussions.

Conclusion

In Africa, communication will improve and mission work thrive when leaders renounce local politics, begin to decentralize functions in their churches and allow information to flow even in their absence. Information sent to our churches through the church leaderships hardly gets down to congregations in time.

We should identify the source of what we do as Christians and find out whether our faith through our commitment to the gospel commands us to do so. Communication should be a subject matter in the curricula of the seminaries where our pastors and bishops are trained.

Every Christian on the continent should see him- or herself as a missionary and, since communication is an ongoing process, education and enlightenment should be a major point in our communication struggle. This will enable Christians to discern facts from opinion in the light of the possibilities provided in the new culture of communication.

Human society is moving quickly to multimedia and multi-sensorial communication through the integration of images, sound and text. Growing alongside this post-literate culture in most mission regions are other cultures which are still oral and literate to various degrees. Therefore, a communication strategy for mission on a continent such as Africa should embrace oral, literate and digital communication.

The political and social problems in Africa have not destroyed her immense and spiritual vitality, and Africa has much to give to the world's Christian faith if we can become strong enough to be left alone to be ourselves, so that what we offer to other churches may be truly African and truly spontaneous.

We must know why we are desperately searching for authenticity in African Christianity. It should be for the glory of God and his mission in Africa and the world. We want to appropriate the Christian faith, but we must speak up and do more than that. This is the time for African Christians to stand up and be counted for the cause of Christ. I don't mean this in the narrow sense in which evangelicals talk about saving the soul.

It is clear from what we observe in Africa that conservative evangelism is downright irrelevant here. In Africa, Christianity will only be credible if Christians will stand firmly by those who are at the moment still fighting for their political liberation and human rights, now being denied them by the black colonizers who have replaced the white (or black) masters.

Christianity will only be relevant in Africa if churches address themselves effectively to the needs in rural development, community health care, family planning and all the other continent's unmet needs. Our missionary approach must save man's soul as well as his body. We need to re-read our scriptures with new eyes and see that God is calling and empowering us to carry out the most difficult and risky task of our mission—that is to speak out for the truth. And to do that, we must be credible ourselves. Our witness to Jesus does not depend on how well we preach the gospel alone, but also on how we live it. Though the "new culture" is strongly determined by technology, it is finally the human person who is decisive. Thus the "witness of life of the individual and Christian communities first and foremost determines mission in social communication." As witnessing, spiritual and liberating people, we also become credible partners for the "new culture" who can help with changes and developments for the good of our continent and humankind.

We must return to the roots—"the fundamentals and essentials of our religion" that bring into focus once again certain values and attitudes that flow from the spiritual characteristics of our cultural heritage. Christian communication should show the value of traditions but at the same time also help to discern new developments in modern communications. African youths need guidance in a diversified society such as the one in which we live. This will help to foster cooperation and unity and balance the extremes emerging in many communities.

We need to change our mindset from the tool orientation in communication which exclusively stresses training as skill orientation to the formation of an inner disposition of openness to listen to God and others. This is a challenge not only for those with a special interest in social communications but for all Christians. The same approach and dimension must also be reflected in all teaching and studying of theology. Thus for us in Africa, when we talk about our daily bread, the issues discussed here and many more readily come to mind. May God help us to overcome.

References

N. Beach, "More to worship than music." *Leadership*, Vol. 26, Issue 4, (2005), 105.

Franz-Josef Eilers: *Communicating between Cultures. An Introduction to Intercultural Communication*. 2nd Edition (Manila: Logos, 1994).

Franz-Josef Eilers, *Communicating in Community, An Introduction to Social Communication*. 3rd revised and enlarged edition (Manila: Logos, 2002), 67f.

Franz-Josef Eilers, *Communicating in Ministry and Mission. An Introduction to Pastoral and Evangelising Communication*. 2nd Edition (Manila: Logos, 2004) (Bangalore, Asian Trading, 2004), 61.

For Encyclical letters on mission see: Raymond Hickey, ed., *Modern Missionary Documents on Africa* (Dublin: Dominican Publications, 1982).

I. de Fijter, "Mainline Religion and Media Culture." Unpublished manuscript, Amsterdam, 2004.

W. Fore, *Television and Religion. The shaping of faith values and culture* (Minneapolis: Augsburg, 1987), 64 ff.

C.F. Harvey, "Technology and the Church through the Centuries." A paper presented at the 25th Annual Conference, Association of Nazarene Sociologists and Researchers, Heritage Center, Kansas City, March 2006

K. L. Kroeker, "Technology and Religion: An Interview with the Episcopal Churches' Tom Ferguson." *TechNews World*, **www.technewsworld.com/story/33078.html**. October 20, 2005

J.H. Nketiah, "Time Contributions of African Culture To Christian Worship." *IRM*, XLVII (1958), 268.

D.F. Noble, *The Religion of Technology: The Divinity Of Man and the Spirit Of Invention*, (New York, NY: Alfred A. Knopf, 1997)

T. Sample, *The Spectacle of Worship in a Wired World* (Nashville, TN: Abingdon Press, 1998).

M. Traber, "Theological Reflections on Communication, Participation and Transformation" in *Group Media Journal*, 1989, 61.

P. Webb, "Symbols for Today's World" in *Media Development*, XXXVI (3), 1989, 21.

Communication Work in the Evangelical Lutheran Church in Tanzania

Elizabeth Lobulu

ELCT Background Information

The Lutheran Church began its activities in Tanzania way back in the 19th century. By 1938, it had grown into seven churches in what was then known as Tanganyika. In 1938, the seven churches formed the Federation of Lutheran Churches in Tanganyika, and on June 19, 1963, under the umbrella of a federation, they merged to become dioceses of a single church known as the Evangelical Lutheran Church in Tanzania (ELCT).

The ELCT currently has a total of 20 dioceses in different parts of the country with a membership of nearly 5.3 million in a population of nearly 38 million people. The Lutherans are the second largest Christian denomination in the country after the Roman Catholic Church.

Church Understanding of Communication

Since its establishment, the mission of the ELCT presupposes its role as a prophetic voice that communicates the gospel in order to promote justice among communities. The ELCT recognizes that achieving the political, economic and social wellbeing necessary for people to be able to live life in all its fullness will come only when the public, policy-makers and communities are all reached with persuasive communication for just action. In its 1994 "Bagamoyo Statement," the church encouraged the use of various media to educate the public and rebuke politicians for their use of immoral methods.

The role of communication as a tool in proclaiming the gospel has been realized since 1932, when the church established its first print organ, *Ufalme wa Mungu*, now *Uhuru na Amani*, in the form of a monthly publication aimed at providing a Christian voice in the struggle for independence. Ever since then, the church has employed both print and electronic media in the form of radio programs, magazines and newsletters to communicate the Good News to the people. Apart from *Uhuru na Amani*, some of the dioceses have their own publications. All church publications are irregular and produced in small quantities due to financial and human resource constraints. *Uhuru na Amani* is a 20-page newsletter in Kiswahili language; it has been operational since 1932, but production is off and on due to inadequate financial and human resources. Two dioceses have magazines of their own—*Ija Webonere* in Bukoba and *Umoja* in Moshi. Again the challenge is how to sustain them financially.

Radio Sauti ya Injili was established as a studio for the Radio Voice of the Gospel (RVOG) based in Addis Ababa from 1962 to 1977. Up to the 1970s, it was very popular among Kiswahili speakers in Eastern, Central and some parts of Southern Africa. It was supported from the beginning by the LWF Development Department, now DMD.

The Vuga Press in Soni in the Tanga Region was started in the 1960s to print church materials including hymn books and by the 1970s it was famous for its quality production. However, the machines have worn out over time and no adequate funds have been located to revive them. On the other hand, the ELCT Northern Diocese has its own print shop which has taken over some of the work that used to be done by *Vuga*, including newsletters and books for the church. It is worth noting that the regional edition of *Lutheran World Information* (*LWI*) for Africa is currently done by the Moshi-based ELCT print shop in Northern Tanzania.

While the performance of some of the older church media systems has deteriorated due to old age, lack of maintenance, lack of funding and enthusiasm, the church has tried to catch up with the technological age advances by installing other modern communication systems such as e-mails and Web sites. All the 20 ELCT dioceses have e-mail connections either through private service providers, cable connection or via satellite, especially for the dioceses that are remotely located. The church-owned Tumaini University and its six constituencies are all connected via internet and they host independent Web sites. The ELCT head office in Arusha has e-mail, internet connection and a Web site for the whole church.

ELCT has what we call common work institutions. These are jointly owned to serve the entire church. One of them is Tumaini University, which has a number of constituent colleges. Other common work institutions are the Mbeya Lutheran Teachers College, Mwanga and Njombe Deaf Schools, Lutheran Junior Seminary in Morogoro, the Lutheran *Radio Sauti ya Injili* in Moshi and the church's head office, based in Arusha.

Within the ELCT structure, the communication desk is under the secretary general's office while radio work is under the Mission and Evangelism department. *Radio Sauti ya Injili* (RSYI)—Kiswahili for "Radio Voice of the Gospel (RVOG)"—started as a studio of the Addis Ababa-based RVOG but began live broadcasting in 1994. Two dioceses—Iringa and Dar es Salaam—have radio stations: *Furaha* FM Radio in Iringa, and *Upendo* FM Radio in Dar es Salaam. Both are still in the infant stage. Located on the slopes of Kilimanjaro, RSYI is the strongest church radio, but due to its topographic/geographical situation, it has not been able to extend its services to other parts of Tanzania. Statistics show coverage only in Kilimanjaro, Arusha, Manyara, Tanga and Dodoma; this has been a challenge for a long time.

ELCT has a Web site. It is currently static, but we plan to have an interactive site in the near future. Visit **www.elct.org** and give us your views! It is expensive to maintain a Web site, but we share the cost across the departments. Although we don't have a permanent staff person to search, update and upload information for the internet, a strategic plan under preparation includes a proposal to employ a contact person for the idea of networking to be realized.

The Communication desk coordinates and facilitates communication and advocacy work in the church.

An Enabling Environment

The Constitution of the United Republic of Tanzania gives citizens the right to freedom of religion, expression, and to seek information and ideas through any medium within and beyond the country provided one does not go against the law. The policy also guarantees non-obstruction of communication flow.

In Dar es Salaam in July 2009, President Jakaya Mrisho Kikwete launched an undersea optic fiber cable that connects South Africa, Mozambique, Tanzania, Kenya and Uganda to Europe and Asia.

With over 4.5 million members, the ELCT has a large potential audience for its radio programs and readership for its publications, including books, news magazines and manuals. But it has been unable to reach this audience due to the dwindling performance of its communication systems. Church leaders' concern about this situation has provoked a variety of measures to address it, including a specific focus on communication as part of the bishops' summit that issued the 1994 Bagamoyo statement; a bishops' consultation held in Momela, Arusha, in 1999; the ELCT communication policy approved by the Executive Council in 2000; the evaluation of the ELCT media organs in 2001; a workshop for ELCT information coordinators held in Arusha in 2007; and the creation of a specific task force on communication in 2007.

The task force commissioned a baseline survey in 2008 on the state of communication in the ELCT, and the formation of a sub-committee to review ELCT communication policy.

Some of the findings of the survey are:

- The church structure does not provide clear direction for communication work.
- Communication activities are dispersed under different units without linkages.
- The *Uhuru na Amani* magazine is produced irregularly and inadequately.
- Most dioceses have old ITC systems and existing computers are inadequate in relation to the number of staff.
- Lack of easy access to the Internet by a majority of staff.
- Lack of computer skills among senior staff.
- Computers are under-utilized in some cases.
- Only four out of 20 dioceses have Web sites.
- Production of SW programs via Trans World Radio (TWR) by *Radio Sauti ya Injili* has been reduced and is now limited to northern Tanzania.
- Lack of human resource management.
- Lack of financial and human resources.
- Lack of full-fledged communication desks/departments.

The findings of the study are guiding the church on the measures to be taken in order to strengthen the communication ministry in the church and all its units.

A draft strategic plan for 2010-2014 has been produced for approval at relevant levels as part of the aforementioned church efforts, and partly in response to the work of the task force.

In March 2000, a strategic planning workshop financially supported by Lutheran Mission Cooperation (LMC) was held in Arusha and attended by participants from various departments and backgrounds. During the workshop, eight themes emerged from a SWOT Analysis. These were: policies/constitution; staffing; resources; capacity-building; ICT; advocacy; operational action-oriented research; and planning and management. In relation to these themes, five priority areas for communication ministry in the ELCT were identified, as follows:

Priority Area 1: Strengthening ELCT communication systems.
Priority Area 2: Improving human resource management.
Priority Area 3: Strengthening financial resource base.
Priority Area 4: Capacity-building in advocacy.
Priority Area 5: Promoting action-oriented research.

The ELCT Vision

A communion of people rejoicing in love and peace, blessed spiritually and physically, hoping to inherit eternal life through Jesus Christ.

The ELCT Mission

To make people know Jesus Christ and have life in its fullness by bringing them the Good News through words and deeds based on the Word of God as it is in the Bible and the Lutheran teachings guided by the ELCT Constitution.

Core Values

The core values that guide ELCT are:

- A witnessing, truthful, advocating, rewarding and daring church.
- Rejoicing and proclaiming salvation.
- Forgiveness and justification by grace through faith in Christ.

Communication Ministry Values

The values that will guide communication ministry are closely aligned and complement the ELCT vision, mission and core values. They are:

- Accountability
- Witnessing to the Good News
- Advocacy
- Freedom of speech
- Ownership of information

The Communication Process Theory

Simply defined, communication is a process in human relations of passing information and understanding from one person to another. We spend about 70 percent of our working hours communicating. Not only in terms of speaking, writing, listening and reading, but also through actions, movements, expressions and gestures.

Other Media

Apart from the mass communication media, including books, newsletters and radio, the church still uses e-mail, slow mail, meetings, landline telephone, fax, radio calls, visits, and mobile phones to communicate horizontally and vertically.

Historical Relations

The ELCT has a long history of relationships in communication ministry with the Lutheran World Federation, and with churches in Germany, Sweden and Denmark, among others. In the 1960s, Radio Voice of the Gospel based in Addis Ababa,

Ethiopia was using English, French and a number of African languages, including Amharic, Hausa and Kiswahili on the SW radio as well as Asian languages.

Examples: The LWI Story

I am privileged to be involved in a *Lutheran World Information* (*LWI*) pilot project involving the local production of an Africa Edition in Tanzania. Through close collaboration between the LWF/OCS, the ELCT and ALCINET, we combine the international *LWI* content with topical issues from churches in the region, sometimes in popular local languages. The aim of the pilot project is to strengthen the self-understanding of LWF in Africa as a communion of churches, and enhance communication between member churches in Africa and stakeholders/partner organizations.

This project was born out of an audit done for OCS and a report to the LWF Council meeting in Lund, Sweden in March 2007. The two-year project is halfway through, and I am its coordinator within the ELCT.

Radio Services in Tanzania 2000 – 2006

TYPE	Commercial	Non-commercial	TOTAL
National Radio	3	2	5
Regional Radio	4	3	7
District Radio	17	18	35
Total	24	23	47

Tanzania Communication Regulatory Authority ©2006

Witnessing Via Radio: Radio and Mobile Phones

The power of radio to deliver messages instantaneously wherever the listener is has been illustrated by its ability even to start new churches. For instance, people in Congo who listened to RVOG and believed in its messages of salvation travelled all the way to Rwanda, thinking the radio was located there. There, they were directed to Dar es Salaam and then Moshi, and they arranged for the church to send missionaries to help in the process of establishing the Lutheran Church in Congo.

Radio is and will continue to be the number one medium of choice for a long time yet in Africa, due to its affordability and the low literacy rate that excludes the majority from acquiring knowledge through printed matter.

Production of printed matter, including magazines, is expensive and the challenge comes in distributing to the rural areas so as to reach members of the congregation on time. The country is huge—about 300,000 sq. km—and there are very few tarmac roads; the majority of people live in areas without road communication during the rainy season.

The Electricity Factor and the Introduction of Mobile Phones

More than 80 percent of the people in Tanzania are not connected to the national electricity grid. In other words, they not only face blackouts, but are also marginalized as far as e-mail and Internet are concerned. Recently, mobile phone services have provided a handy alternative: people are now able to send cellular phone text messages (SMS) to inform and make business enquiries without the need to travel as they had to in the past.

Percentage of mobile phone users 2000 – 2008

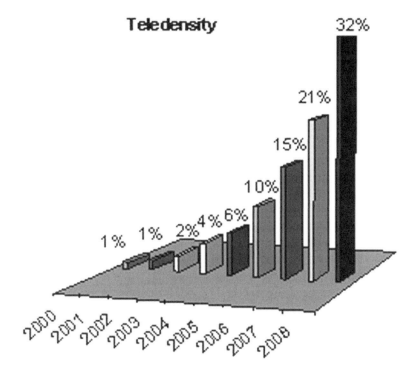

(Source of Population Data: National Bureau of Statistics Projections)

Poverty and Sustainability

In Africa, the most active church members are women, and it is an open secret that women are the poorest of the poor in our society. If their contributions are too small, it is also because their ability to contribute toward the running of the church or development activities is very low. The church is, therefore, over-dependent on donor funding to establish major projects such as communication infrastructure and management.

Through bilateral arrangements and partners including the LWF and the LMC through multilateral arrangements, sister churches have been generous enough to support churches in Africa to establish media houses including radio stations, newsletters and Web sites in order to sustain the communication flow.

However the ever-rising costs and the revamping of partner organizations means that the level of funding too is going down as a whole, while the slice earmarked for communication work is also dwindling drastically year after year. In early 2000, ELCT units including the dioceses went through a reorganization in which some units had to be eliminated and the majority of the people working in communication were removed from their positions. Toward the beginning of 2006, the church and its stakeholders felt the pinch and discussed it openly.

Outcome of the SWOT Analysis

The ELCT Constitution has a clause that states categorically that the presiding bishop is the chief spokesman of the church. It thus restricts the mandate to issue statements and information to the public. But interpretation varies. If it suits a leader of one of the 20 autonomous dioceses, he may speak on behalf of his diocese without any hindrance. But when the secretary general speaks in a diocese, he will sometimes encounter a problem. I would urge that the current review of the 2000 ELCT Communication Policy clarify the rules regarding other spokespeople in addition to the chief spokesperson so as not to curtail freedom of expression and people's right to information.

Secondly, there is the issue of government policy on communication. Although it encourages people to invest in the rural areas, the government was also limiting radio station coverage to only five of the 20 regions on Tanzania's mainland, for example. The policy now allows nation-wide coverage using MW transmitters, but the extremely high cost of electricity discourages investment in MW.

A new policy in the making may restrict the number of media organs that an organization can have. This discussion is on-going.

During the SWOT analysis, it was felt that there was a need to establish a network of communicators to promote information-sharing. But the study showed that less than 25 percent of dioceses had an information or communication unit in place. There can be no network if there is no one to network with!

The issue of ICT use was also discussed. As usual, the best equipment and the best computers in particular would be on the bishop's or the secretary general's desk. Most of them travel a lot, but that may not be a huge problem. The problem is that some of the leaders lack computer skills and have to wait for their secretaries to open and print e-mails before they can act on them. These are examples of a failure to take advantage of the 21st century IT development leap in Internet and digital communication technology.

Voice Telecommunication Subscribers in Tanzania (2000 - 2008)

Year	2000	2001	2002	2003	2004	2005	2006	2007	2008
Fixed Lines	173,591	177,802	161,590	147,006	148,360	154,420	151,644	163,269	123,809
Mobile	126,646	275,560	606,859	1,295,000	1,942,000	3,389,787	5,614,922	8,322,857	13,006,793
Total	300,237	453,362	768,449	1,442,006	2,090,360	3,544,207	5,766,566	8,486,126	13,130,602
Mobile Share	42%	61%	79%	90%	93%	96%	97%	98%	99%

Source: Tanzania Communications Regulatory Authority ©2008

Mobile Phones

Mobile phones have become very useful and popular in Africa. Let me give you a few examples. According to a recent study reported in *The Nation* newspaper, there are 17 million mobile phones in Kenya (1:2 Kenyans). The phones are not only used to make calls and exchange SMS messages to enhance business and encourage economic growth, but also as radio to tune in to FM stations around big towns or cities. As the table above shows, 99 percent of all voice telecommunication in Tanzania is done using mobile phones. The phones are also being used to pay electricity bills and, with the coming of *MPesa* (money transfers), people can effect financial transactions using mobile phones the way bank accounts operate.

Conclusion

In many respects, the communication future looks bleak for the church in Tanzania. But given the progress in ICT, including use of mobile phones to phone-in and enliven radio programs; the introduction of a fast connection optic fibre linking Europe, Asia and Africa; the fact that the RVOG showed that it is possible to pool resources for a powerful medium of gospel and evangelism propagation that could go beyond borders, as churches in Africa and the LWF as a global communion, we are now more than before challenged to exploit the radio option once again. When radio is developed, the rest of the media will also progress by tapping in on satellite, radio, internet, optic fibre and TV to ensure people get their spiritual *daily bread.*

References:

Bagamoyo Statement on Economic and Political Democracy
ELCT Communication Policy of 2000
ELCT Communication Strategic (Draft) Plan 2010-2014
ELCT Constitution
Prof. Leonidas Kalugila, Th.D., *"Uongozi wa Kanisa,"* (Arusha: The Lutheran Heritage Foundation, 2001)
National ICT Policy of 2003
Tanzania Broadcasting Services Act of 1993
Tanzania Communication Regulatory Authority Act of 2003
Tanzania Communications Act of 1993

Asia

Communication as a Mission and Ministry of the Church – An Asian Perspective

Daniel Kirubaraj

1. Introduction

Communicating the good news of God's salvation is a divine and human event. The church's communication as a mission and ministry has its roots in Jesus and is shared unto the ends of the earth within the authority of Jesus' great commandment,[1] given to his disciples. The Orthodox Church tradition claims that of the twelve disciples, St Thomas, the doubting disciple-apostle, brought God's mission to the Asian continent and as far as India as early as the first century.[2] Since then, the Asian church lives her faith through word and deed within Asia's diverse socio-cultural contexts.

Communication and daily bread remain day-to-day human community experiences. The stark reality of the present imbalanced communication and bread-sharing systems obviously deny humanity a balanced socio-religious community experience. On the one hand, in the *techno-econo*[3] information-based world, humans lack communion and daily bread. On the other hand, many others suffer from information overflow and excess food. Hence, communication and daily bread have become the subjects of a struggle between life and death due to unequal sharing in day-to-day community life. The "obese" and "emaciated" natures of communication found in the church's mission and ministry also seem to resist Christ's model of communication that leads to a life-sharing communion and reflects Trinity community action.

[1] Ref. Matthew 28:18-20.

[2] **http://enwikipedia.org/wiki/Thomas_the Apostle**. Main page.

[3] As preferred by the author to denote "Technological and economical."

To reflect on the theme *from an Asian perspective* in the ambiguous communication contexts of our contemporary world implies that we must take sides with the technologically deprived and yet culturally rich communities of Asia. In doing so, this paper considers certain communication barriers involved in the church's mission and ministry, proposes a yardstick of communication theology as culture and as a life-sharing process obligatory for mission and ministry at global and local levels.

2. Understanding Communication

Before proceeding further, we will consider two stories that may help to sharpen the reader's methodological understanding of communication. The first story aims to question whether the *universal* meaning of communication as the church's mission and ministry is widely understood, thus avoiding certain regional, contextual, practical, technological and theological biases or reservations. The second story aims to propose that a communion culture is the first and foremost core value of church communication, and that popular *techno-econo* mass communication methodologies are of secondary importance. We shall thus endeavor to retrieve[4] the complete meaning of communication with its cultural value. Essentially, it remains a life-sharing community experience, a fusion of true and subjective community identity which has universal value within church communication as her mission and ministry. Such communication has been patterned, apparently modelled and theologically claimed in Jesus' saying: *I am the way, the truth and the life.*[5]

Story one: Five visually challenged friends wished to understand what an elephant is. Given the opportunity to touch an elephant, the first friend touched its legs and decided that an elephant resembles a pillar. A second laid his hands on the elephant's trunk and assumed that an elephant resembles a pestle. The third patted the elephant's stomach and marvelled that an elephant was like a wall. The fourth fingered its ear and guessed that an elephant is like a colander. The last toyed with its tail and compared the elephant to a broom. Having finished their individual observations, the friends began to discuss their understandings of the elephant. Disappointingly, each one stuck to his own partial understanding. They began to disagree with one another and thus completely failed to understand what a whole elephant looks like.

---

[4] To negate meta-cultural aspects imposed in the understanding of communication.
[5] Ref. John 14:6.

We wonder whether only partial visions of communication as a mission and ministry of the church have been advocated from different contexts. However, the above story invites churches in different contexts to admit an holistic understanding of communication. Further, this paper invites them to achieve such communication through exploring certain answers to the question: Why communication? Our paper also attempts to add praxis values of communication as the church's mission and ministry.

Story two: Once upon a time, in a small and remote village, a king who miserably failed to master archery was astonished to see a number of arrows shot accurately at the core of some target boards. Curious to meet such an expert archer, he was very surprised to be presented with a small boy. "How could you aim so accurately?" the king asked the boy. "It's easy really," the boy replied, explaining, "I shoot the arrow first and then draw circles around it." This story might be a bit silly, yet it gives us the clue that there might be a simple and commonly shared communication method as a way of life, a cultural reality within our day-to-day community communion experience.

A heart generous enough to accept such a simple communication principle might perhaps be what the church needs to solve her unresolved communication problems. In our opinion, it is high time that the church turns from expounding a technology-based informative communication approach and adopts a positive and God-intended scheme of communication in which sharing life itself will be the core value. Interestingly, any norms that hinder the sharing of life, procreation of "species"[6] and the performance of community activity could be considered sinful.

Etymologically, "communication" is rooted in the Latin *communis*, which means "common." Its verb, *communicare*, means "to transmit," "to share" and "to establish a community."[7] "Communicare" and its cognates are rooted in the older Latin word *munus*, and it refers to "public duty."[8] Words like "common," "communion" and "community" are rooted in the Greek *koinonia*, a parallel to "communis."[9] Thus, "communication is a deeply religious event."[10] To be

---

[6] C.R.W. David, ed., *Communication in Theological Education: A Curriculum*. Bangalore:Board of Theological Education of the Senate of Serampore College (1988) 7.

[7] Michael Traber, "Theological Reflections on Communication, Participation and Transformation" in *Group Media Journal*, 1989, 61; and Peter Elvy, *The Future of Christian Broadcasting in Europe* (London: McCrimmons, 1990) 1.

[8] Keyan G. Tomaselli and Arnold Shepperson, "Resistance Through Mediated Orality." In Stewart. M. Hoover and Knut Lundby, eds., *Rethinking Media, Religion and Culture* (New Delhi: SAGE, 1997), 218.

[9] Richard. A. Muller, *Dictionary of Latin and Greek Theological Terms* (Grand Rapids: Baker Book House Company, 1985) 75 & 169.

[10] Pauline Webb, "Symbols for Today's World" in *Media Development*, XXXVI (3) (1989) 21.

holistic in mission and ministry, the church needs to involve God-intended functional meanings, namely culture, ethics and theology.

2.1 Communication as a Mission of the Church

The Online Etymology Dictionary defines "mission" as derived from the Latin word *missionem* which means the "act of sending" and *mittrer* denoting "to send."[11] *Mission* is the act of sending or the state of being sent or delegated by authority with certain powers for transacting business.[12] Communication as a church's mission is essentially *Missio Dei*,[13] a Latin Christian theological term that refers to the very nature of God.[14]

Communication as God's mission began with God and was revealed in the event of creation. The communion-centred communication between the Creator and the creation helps us return to the blending of the theological, cultural and ethical essences of communication with special reference to the Trinity attribute of God, Son and Spirit in the church's mission and ministry today.[15]

Theologically, in answer to the *Why?* aspect of communication, we can say that in the creation event,[16] God communicated with God's self and created all those who exist to *be* and to *become in communion* with God's self and with other selves. Culturally, the *How?* values of God-intended communication as a life-sharing experience among all living beings have been situated within the procreative process: *God blessed them, and God said unto them, be fruitful, and multiply, and replenish the earth, and subdue it: and have dominion over the fowl of the air, and over every living thing that moves upon the earth.*[17] Accordingly, overall God-intended communication as mission can be understood as a definite, ongoing *universal and vertical*[18] life-sharing process. Ethically, God's mission and ministry in Jesus' incarnation model of communication calls for the blending of God's message and the medium[19] in the word that became flesh[20] and the

---

[11] www.etymoline.com/index.php?term=mission.

[12] http://ardictionar.com/Mission/5550.

[13] A term coined in1934 by Karl Hartenstein, a German missiologist, as response to Karl Barth's *actioDei* (Latin for "the action of God").

[14] http://en.wikipedia.org/wiki/Missio_dei

[15] http://en.wikipedia.org/wiki/Missio_dei

[16] Ref. Genesis chapter 1.

[17] Ref. Genesis 1:28.

[18] To be understood as "time and space"-bound experience of sharing life always and everywhere.

[19] Marshall McLuhan, *Understanding Media: The Extensions of Man* (New York: Mentor, 1964).

[20] Ref. John 1:1 & 14.

way it helps humans to commune with God.[21] Jesus' model of communication redefines the communication ethics of the church's mission and ministry in terms of integrating her message into real life, fulfilling the divine-human-human communication as communion and not merely as information.

2.2 Communication: Asian Theories

Communication in Asia includes several Asian communication theories, such as Chinese, Islamic, Japanese, Indian and indigenized Western ones. These Asian communication theories are constructed to suit cultural milieus, the role of religion, media, power politics and the search for Asian identities in communication and so on. In an effort to capture this scenario, Xu Xiaoge,[22] summarizes struggles involved in Asian communication perspectives relating to press systems, communication ethics, professional standards and the trends and strategies of future Asian communication, and adds that the values of Asian communication have always been compared with Western journalistic cultural, theoretical standards.[23]

This tendency raises concerns about the local and universal nature of the future Asian communication experience. In addition to this legitimate concern, Asian economic and political crises, the increasing domination of Western media giants, and the unbalanced global information flow have also affected the transparency of Asian communication.

The above-mentioned situation in turn has caused grave concern about the need to safeguard the cultural identities of Asian communication in the battle against Western cultures and values. Referring to Chu, Xiaoge critically observes that Western communication theories do not fully describe, explain or predict the communication phenomenon in Asia. It is pointed out that Western communication theories have been limited to quantitative methods, lack focus, are too repetitive and weak in studies of structure and the function of communication in social contexts, and do not regard culture as a critical factor in communication.

Strengthening the Asian perspective on communication, Xiaoge[24] suggests that Western-oriented communication theories can be enriched by using Asian communication processes, behavior patterns and experiences. To support his argument, Xiaoge reasons that Asian communication perspectives include

---

[21] Ref. John 14:6.

[22] Xu Xiaoge, "Asian Perspectives in Communication: Assessing the Search." [Online] Accessed 19 February 2010. **www.acjournal.org/holdings/vol3/Iss3/spec1/Xiaoge.html**

[23] Xu Xiaoge. Asian Perspectives in Communication (2010).

[24] Xu Xiaoge, Asian Perspectives in Communication (2010).

development values, such as the desire for harmony or to avoid differences and conflicts, and emphasize the role of the educator and catalyst of social and political changes in society. We agree with Xiaoge that the strengths and weaknesses of Asian and Western communication perspectives challenge the church to revitalize communication in her mission and ministry so as to restore an appropriate and responsible community identity to humanity.

3. Communication and Human Identity

In the world of mass communication and information technology, a few human beings coin messages, give them meaning, and share them with millions of other humans using different tools and media in different contexts. In this context, communication depends heavily on the use of non-human technical devices. Seldom do humans as a community share responsibility for coining the messages and ascribing meaning to them. These communication ambiguities seem to arise from the basic hypothesis upon which human beings base their identity. In his book *Communication of the Christian Faith*, Hendrik Kraemer characterizes the ambiguous human situation as "knowing yet not knowing one's self, knowing and yet not knowing each other."[25] Kraemer has pinpointed the problem that not only gradually slowed down the church's communication but also rendered the communication theology from which the church's God-human-human communication identity needs to be derived less clear.

3.1 The Western Approach
According to Adam and Tannery, Rene Descartes' *Cogito ergo sum*, that is, "I think therefore I am" establishes reasoning power as the core of humanness and human (communication) activity.[26] This view seems to sharply divide humanity from the rest of living beings by claiming superiority over them, and it divides humans themselves into intellectuals and non-intellectuals. These assumptions are indeed in opposition to certain basic assumptions on human communication enabling the individual to *be* in *his/herself*, and in the communion of individuals to *become* a *communed community* of selves.

---

[25] Hendrik Kraemer, *The Communication of the Christian Faith*, 7th edition (London: Lutterworth Press, 1957), 14.

[26] Charles Adam and Paul Tannery, eds., *The Philosophical Writings of Descartes*, trans., John Cottingham and Robert Stoothoff, (Paris: J. Vrin, 1904), 25.

For Western scholars like Robert K. Merton,[27] the *self-fulfilling prophecy* helps to shape human identity not only by one's own action but also by the reaction of others. Thus, a "socially reduced me" not only breaks communication between humans, but their very life. Self involves a *sense of competence* and balances competence with expectation;[28] the sense *of self-determination* is the sense of being in charge of our lives; the *sense of togetherness* includes a basic and consistent belief, emotions and so on; and a *sense of moral goodness* is an ethical validation.[29]

3.2 The African Approach

In Third World contexts, for example in South Africa, a person identifies his/her "self" in the community context. Such a concept is known as *Ubuntu*, which strongly binds the self with the "community" in which one identifies one's self through relating with responsible others; it claims, "I am what I am because of others." The essence of *Ubuntu* is that "persons depend on responsible persons to be persons."[30]

South African Bishop Desmond Tutu defines the concept of *Ubuntu* as the heart of many African cultures; *I am because we are, in which the human expression derives itself in relation with others*. Tutu further affirms *a deep sense of belonging and communion, the conviction of shared humanity as the basis for life and survival*.[31] Surely, the African insight on human identity culls out the cultural nature of communication and moves far beyond a community-dividing intellectual human experience. However, in our opinion, it lacks the overall universal communication community possibility whose theological essence would make it a complete communication model.

3.3 The Asian Approach

Asian philosophy in general, and the Eastern philosophy of communication in particular, insist upon the whole: "The unity of substance and form, reason and experience, and knowledge and action."[32] It unfolds its results in a natural

---

[27] Robert K. Merton, *Social Theory and Social Structure* (New York: Free Press, 1957).

[28] William James, *Psychology: The Briefer Course* (New York: Henry Holt, 1892), 187-188.

[29] Em Griffin, *A First Look at Communication Theory* (New Delhi: McGraw-Hill, Inc., 1991), 70-75.

[30] Augustine Shutte, *Ubuntu: An Ethic for a New South Africa* (Pietermaritzburg: Cluster Publications, 2001), 3.

[31] Ref. LWF Guiding Principles for Comprehensive Communication, 'A Communicative Communion', Draft January 2003, 3.

[32] Shelton Gunaratne, "Asian Approaches to Communication Theory." In *Media Development*, XXVII (1) (1988), 53.

process and requires deeper analysis of such community collectivity. It aims at a liberation of "being one and the whole" and views language as inadequate to bring the meaning of the ultimate reality to those who involve themselves in communication.[33]

Emotions play a vital role in the Eastern-Indian models of communication. Human relationships based on mutual dependence become the basis of communication.[34] Jayaweera asserts: *Indians do not need to construct new paradigms. They have an inexhaustible reservoir of alternative models within their own history.*[35]

However, the negative roles communication plays in the Indian hierarchically structured caste system cannot be compared favorably to Western individual-based freedom, because both the Indian hierarchical and the dominant Western paradigms separate one person from another.

The Western, African and Asian assumptions of human identity extracted from communication perspectives seem to lack a certain basic hypothesis of human communication and its theological nucleus. For example, as we noted in relation to the African experience, the inherent *intra-* and *inter-*communed human identity, with or without "thinking capacity" remains the individual, the *being*. The existing *self* also remains the community, the *becoming* self of the community already in communion.

Theologically, such identity began with God's creation event and continued always and everywhere within the human as well as all existing and co-existing species within the procreation process. We continue to stress that the church needs a new, more human and praxis model of communication, that could be based on a synthesis of the Western, African and Asian/Eastern communication models.

Humans whether in the West or the East communicate on two planes, namely the vertical and the horizontal. Vertically, we communicate with God above and with God's subordinates and other creatures below. Horizontally, we communicate with other human beings like ourselves.[36] This could be understood as the framework of "holistic communication" or "communication theology" fulfilled in Jesus' model of communication in his mission and ministry. It could provide a complete communication model for the church

[33] Wimal Dissanayake, ed., *Communication Theory: The Asian Perspective* (Singapore: AMIC, 1988), 39-55.

[34] Yum quoted in D. Lawrence Kincaid, ed., *Communication Theory: Eastern and Western Perspectives* (San Diego: Academic Press Inc., 1987), 87-100.

[35] Wimal Dissanayake, *Communication Theory: The Asian Perspective*, 66.

[36] V. Devasahayam, ed., *Frontiers of Dalit Theology* (Madras: ISPCK, 1997), 279.

in her mission and ministry to share the truth, which is also the way and the life[37] with every generation.

4. Communication as a Mission and Ministry of the Church

Communication as a mission and ministry of the church in the Asian context is not exempted from the constraints discussed in the above section. Its complexity includes Asian religious pluralistic traditions,[38] information technologies,[39] theological dispositions[40] and so forth. In order to overcome theoretical, cultural, religious and media power conflicts, and ethical, economical and political crises, we will explore a Jesus model of communication for the church to implement in her mission and ministry. On this subject, Roberto C. Mallari[41] writes:

> ... the church should stress always (that) traditional means of communication, which have grown over centuries in culture are the very foundation of communication. A spirituality, which flows out of the communication of the Holy Trinity, must be reflected in and matched with deep daily experiences of the communicators in the church. It is a spirituality marked with a deep commitment to experiencing the message giver (Triune God), the message (God's Love), and the way of witnessing and sharing the message.

Mallari's observation seems to echo our thoughts. Around the world today, church communication as a mission and ministry seems to be based on information technologies, bound by media influence, and assessed quantitatively. Where this is the case, this bias has emptied the church's mission and ministry of Jesus' model of communication.

4.1 Jesus' Model of Communication

Though an ordinary man from Galilee and a carpenter's son, Jesus adopted a complete communication model in his mission and ministry. People witnessed

---

[37] Ref. John 14:6.

[38] Franz-Josef Eilers, ed., *Social Communication in Religious Traditions in Asia*, Vol.7. (Manila: Logos, 2005).

[39] Franz-Josef Eilers, ed., *E-Generation. The Communication of Young People in Asia: Concern of the Church*, Vol.4. (Manila: Logos, 2003).

[40] Franz-Josef Eilers, ed., *Social Communication Formation in Priestly Ministry*, Vol.2. (Manila: Logos, 2002).

[41] **www.docstoc.com/docs/20157453/The Church-and Social-Communication-in-Asia**

that *He wasn't like the teachers of the Law; instead he taught with authority.*[42] Jesus' model of communication qualitatively and fully imbibed cultural, ethical and theological values. Firstly, Jesus multiplied his "I" identity as the shared image of God, essentially the cultural milieu of God's Trinity community. Secondly, Jesus' God-to-human and human-to-human relationship demonstrated the ethical authority in his communication. Thirdly, Jesus affirmed the theological niche in his model of communication through his subjective experience of the Trinity community communion.[43]

Jesus' model of communication differed from that of his contemporaries. Unlike Jesus, the scribes and Pharisees neither communed with God nor with their fellow human beings. Hence, their communication was unauthentic, un-realistic and hampered by communication barriers. We fear that church communication too may experience such barriers in her mission and ministry.

4.2 Barriers to Church Communication

In the light of Jesus' model of communication, we propose that the church's day-to-day communication as a mission and ministry in no way needs to restrain its cultural, ethical and theological authenticity. Authentic church communication need not yield to ambiguous cultural constraints, propelled by meta-values and belittled as constructive contradiction. To do so is to submit to three main barriers to the church's communication as mission and ministry, namely:

- dominant religious communication attitudes which relate to cultural values;
- the commercial and political communication dogmas which link ethical issues; and
- the denial of theological experience as communication of the faithful, and which minimize the God-human-human relationship.

These three barriers will be further defined below.

4.2.1 Dominant Religious Communication Attitudes

With reference to the historical background of Jesus' communication model, the dominant traditional religious communication practices of the Old Testament religious leaders[44] essentially focused on the methods by which God

---

[42] Ref. Matthew 7:29.

[43] Ref. Matthew 28:18-20.

[44] Scribes, Priests and Pharisees.

was to be worshipped. This tradition emphasized communication as teaching of biblical texts and their interpretation; and did not involve God-intended life-sharing communion, essentially the God-communed-cultural experience. In such a communication process, the priests as opinion leaders positioned themselves as the sole agents and center of religious communication. Thus, the dominant religious communication denied the God-shared "I" in which God's community culture is rooted. Jesus communicated and taught authoritatively against these hypocritical and evil-minded religious leaders.[45] Some anxiety exists that practices similar to those that were dominant in Jesus' time may prevail in church communication in its mission and ministry today.

Tillich[46] was of the opinion that such a situation prevailed in the churches of his day. He argued that the language and symbols of religious systems need to be transparent to their believers. Enlightened theologians like Tillich, Schmude and others demanded that communication in the church's mission and ministry reflect on God and on God's characteristics that relate humans with God. They posited a continuing need to re-value religious symbols.[47] We too feel that there is a dire need that requires an urgent and careful response involving the communion of the church with God and with people. Neglecting this duty could only strengthen the barriers to the church's community communication on economic and political dominance and divisions.

4.2.2 Economic and Political Influences

The second barrier that corrupts the religious meanings of the symbols, sacrifices and offerings used in the church's mission and ministry involves the impact on them of corrupt economic and political activities. Jesus condemned the commercial and politically based activities going on in Jerusalem's Temple. The sacrifices offered there converted it from a place of worship, a communing experience with God and God' people, into a market place and a den of thieves.[48] The emphasis on commercial and political endeavours contradicted the real meaning of those symbols, such as the abiding presence of Yahweh, the Holiness of God and the liberating experience of God from any type of slavery.

The present communication context of the churches, including the symbols and sacraments, seem to be loaded with doctrinal and ritual values that sup-

---

[45] Ref. Matthew Chapter 23.

[46] Paul Tillich, "The Nature of Religious Language." In Robert Kimball, C. Robert, eds., *Theology of Culture* (New York: Oxford University Press, a Galaxy Book, 1964), 53-67.

[47] Paul A. Soukup, *Communication and Theology: Introduction and Review of the Literature* (London: WACC, 1983) 32-33.

[48] Ref. Luke 19:45-46.

port the priests' political, social and economic dominance and their concerns, such as maintaining the status quo, the church hierarchy and administrative systems. They seem to help, in turn, to maintain a certain dominant model of communication, to deny the communion experience to the simple and faithful who are reduced to the status of passive consumers of words preached.

Theologically trained priests also seem to be opinion leaders of the faithful in matters of faith and morals. It is still such priests who hold the key to interpret and to "offer hope of renewing the discourse of Christian community with others."[49] Dillistone[50] studied the symbol system in the churches in detail and argued that they are still the offshoots of Western culture with topological, chronological, societal and psycholinguistic characteristics[51] that cannot but support the globalization that controls today's world, and that they lack the "relationship"-based religious communication that Jesus, his disciples and the Apostle Paul used.

4.2.3 Denial of Theological Experience

The third barrier culled from reflection on Jesus' model of communication is a refusal to recognize that *all* the faithful, including the common people, are capable of theological experience. This refusal implies that personal faith experience is reserved exclusively to the privileged and to their intellectual realm. The important theological fact that Jesus, God's Word,[52] who became flesh and himself was considered in his time as one among the many common people (*hoi polloi*),[53] has been forgotten. Jesus himself condemned such an exclusive attitude as sin and hypocrisy and not only warned people against such teachers of the law and the Pharisees, but also predicted their punishment.[54]

Hence, remarks Kramer, it was in Jesus Christ that the inner motives and the ambiguous human communication situation were perfectly illustrated. Kramer calls Jesus the word, the symbol par excellence of human interactive communication.[55] On the one hand, the word, Jesus, remains a symbol of truth that forms the subject matter of both communication and theology and, on the other hand, "Jesus" has been accepted by many common people, resonates in their mouths, and

---

[49] Ludek Broz, "Hermeneutics and Forgiveness." In *Theology Digest*, 21,1, (1979) 33-36.

[50] F.W. Dillistone, *Traditional Symbols and the Contemporary World* (London: Epworth Press, 1973).

[51] Paul A. Soukup, *Communication and Theology*, 35.

[52] Ref. John 1:1.

[53] Ref. John 1:14.

[54] Ref. Matthew, Chapter 23.

[55] Hendrik Kramer, *The Communication of the Christian Faith*, 14.

is part of their community lives day in and day out. And in this, many common people have found their theological way and life in Jesus.[56]

We propose that the above-mentioned theological experience needs to be the foundation for the church's complete communication model. This model can provide the needed strength and theoretical framework for a communication theology, and invigorate the church's mission and ministry. It would constitute an authentic alternative to the present church communication attitude dependent upon and biased by *techno-econo* mass communication rather than the ardently sought communication theology.

5. Communication Theology

Communication theology is not a hair-splitting mental gymnastic. It is not a mere toying with words and concepts inside the four walls of a classroom in a theological college[57] but rather a praxis, a core event, in which communication and theology must mutually enrich each other and enhance the quality of the "communication language of the faithful."[58]

Soukup writes that "No one is clear about where the line between communication and theology should be drawn."[59] McDonnell[60] suggests a merger of two terms, i.e., communication and theology, to enhance a mutual reflection in the light of Christian faith. However, he is cautious about the generalizing of anything as communication and theology.[61] This seems to indicate a fear of accepting communication as a process, a relation and a content, which in fact makes it holistic and theological. Karl Rahner calls it "the self communication of God."[62]

5.1 Communication Theology: Church's Mission and Ministry

Our Trinity community God is a God who communes and communicates within God's self. This self-communicating God also communicates beyond God's self through Jesus, the incarnated Word and the empowering Spirit of God.

---

[56] Ref. John 14:6.

[57] Paul A. Soukup, *Communication and Theology*, 75.

[58] Joseph Palakeel, "Communications and Theological Formation." In Joseph Palakeel, ed., *Towards a Communication Theology* (Bangalore, India: Asian Trading Corporation, 2003), 12.

[59] Paul A.Soukup, *Communication and Theology*, 19.

[60] James McDonnell, *Theology and Communication: A Bibliography Compiled by the Centre for the Study of Communication and Culture* (London: The Centre for the Study of Communication and Culture, 1982), 1.

[61] James Mc Donnell in Paul A.Soukup's *Communication and Theology*, 19.

[62] Paul A.Soukup, *Communication and Theology*, 20.

The communicating God remains in communion with the whole creation. God communes with the creation because God cares to impart God's communicating nature with humankind. God's nature of sharing and caring for life through the creation and procreation process has a certain theological impact on communication. Such God-initiated, Jesus-fulfilled and Holy Spirit-guided church communication as mission and ministry determines communication theology.

God extended God's community to creation by breathing God's breath through the spoken word.[63] God breathed God's Spirit into the hand-made human, and the human became a living being.[64] Thus, since creation, God's mission, the *missio dei*, began as the *communis*: the commonly shared God's "I" with all other "I"-s, humankind. Since then, God's mission remains as God's community action, in which God's "I" and the other "I"-s share. In other words, God's community action remains as "communication theology." It is precisely such divine-human community interaction initiated by the Trinity community God that forms the authentic ground of the church's mission and ministry.

The authenticity of communication theology within the church's mission and ministry could be drawn from God's authority over the creation in general and humans in particular. God authoritatively committed the creation "to be" and "to become" and to be God's community within a set world order of a communion culture and with a certain ethical responsibility for preserving the lives meant to be the bread for life:

> Be fruitful, and multiply; fill the earth, subdue it; have dominion [...] See, I have given you every herb that yields seed which is on the face of all the earth, and every tree whose fruit yields seed; to you it shall be for food. Also, to every beast of the earth, to every bird of the air, and to everything that creeps on the earth, in which there is life, I have given every green herb for food.[65]

Since then, the creation seems to be struggling to be God's community and demonstrate God's community action, communication theology, within a set procedure or world order; to share the purpose and benefit of life as the divine-nature-human culture from within and with all. At this juncture, one needs to recognize the core value of "communication theology."

In simple words, communication theology is "the beautiful fusion of God's history with the history of the creation" affirmed with God's commission to

---

[63] Ref. Genesis.1:3, 6, 9, 11, 14, 20, 24 & 26.

[64] Ref. Genesis. 1:26-28; 2:7, 18 -22.

[65] Ref. Genesis 1:28-30.

humankind. Communication theology thus manifests its in-depth authority and possible diversified communication phenomena. Communication theology, as a process, remains an ongoing conglomeration of God's cognition, and synthesizes different forms of life that coexist in the universe within and beyond human knowledge; it remains as the universal life-sharing paradigm.

The paradigm of communication theology involves Jesus as the culmination of God-human shared communication as church's mission and ministry. God the *sender* shared God's life—theologically, the message—via the *channel* of Jesus to the church *receiver* to certain universal, eternal and communion *effect*. Jesus, the spoken and incarnated word of God, also became the God-shared bread of life.[66] Thus, the uniqueness of this paradigm, which fuses Jesus Christ with the church's mission and ministry, life and life-giving bread, the promised symbol of God's shared life.[67]

Communication theology, when adopted in the church's mission and ministry, cuts across the human-made cultural, ethical and theological limitations that bind the church's mission and ministry, and offers God-intended meanings to them. Culturally, it maintains procreation possibilities, brings life into existence and remains as God's approved way of continuing God's shared life. Ethically, communication theology guides us to handle the communication issues posed as Bachman's "constructive contradiction."[68] Thus, it is God's method of dividing the false from the "true." Theologically, it puts God the creator in communion with God's creation.

Conclusion

Communication and daily bread remain an ambiguous, human day-to-day community experience. The church's communication as a mission and ministry needs to be redeemed from the present dominant, information-based, metacultural and dividing models and theories of communication. In such an effort, the church—as the community called to communicate a new world order of communication in her communication as a mission and ministry—needs to practice Jesus' model of complete communication. This model involves cultural, ethical and theological values. Such values within the church's mission and

---

[66] Ref. John 6:35.

[67] Ref. John 3:16.

[68] As mentioned in Karin Achtelstetter's *"Communication in the LWF: A Constructive Contradiction?"* Paper presented at Erlangen, 17-21 June 2009, 8-9.

ministry generate not a mere abstract universal model of communication but a subjective intra- and inter-divine-nature-human experience that contains the intrinsic values of communication theology; the divine-human-human experience within the church's communication as a mission and ministry; and a unique model in being and becoming one in the other. Isaiah offered a vision for such church communication—our daily bread—with definite mission and ministry mandates, and predicted:

> The wolf also shall dwell with the lamb,
> And the leopard shall lie down with the kid;
> and the calf and the young lion and the fatling together;
> and a little child shall lead them.
> And the cow and the bear shall feed; their young ones shall lie down together;
> and the lion shall eat straw like the ox.
> And the sucking child shall play on the hole of the asp,
> And the weaned child shall put his hand on the cockatrice' den.
> They shall not hurt nor destroy in all my holy mountain:
> For the earth shall be full of the knowledge of the Lord,
> as the waters cover the sea.[69]

---

[69] Ref. Isaiah.11:6-9.

Latin America and the Caribbean

Challenges for Communication in the Evangelical Church of the Lutheran Confession in Brazil

Jaime Jung

The Evangelical Church of the Lutheran Confession in Brazil (Igreja Evangé-lica de Confissão Luterana no Brasil – IECLB) is a member of the Lutheran World Federation. Subdivided into 18 synods, with about 715,000 members, 400 parishes and 1,800 congregations, it is the largest Lutheran church in South America and has its origins with the German immigrants in the 19th century. Once predominantly rural, the IECLB membership has increasingly been drawn to the bigger cities. Its primary ministries are mission, service, education, communication and ecumenical relations. The development of new congregations has been on the increase over recent years. The active church workers are pastors, catechists, diaconal workers and missionaries—and one third of these workers are women.

In recent years, the IECLB has provided missionary outreach programs in Northern Brazil and in urban areas, as well as diaconal services with landless people, small farmers, indigenous peoples and street children.[1] Its priorities and challenges include confessional unity in the context of religious pluralism, the public responsibility of the IECLB within Brazilian society, dialogue with internal evangelical, charismatic movements as well as with the PPL-*Pastoral Popular Luterana* (representing mainly liberation theology), themes related to faith and money, stewardship, financial autonomy on all levels and HIV/AIDS.[2]

---

[1] www.elca.org/Who-We-Are/Our-Three-Expressions/Churchwide-Organization/Global-Mission/Where-We-Work/Latin-America-Caribbean/Brazil.aspx

[2] www.oikoumene.org/de/mitgliedskirchen/regionen/lateinamerika/brasilien/evangelische-kirche-lb-in-brasilien.html

Communication in the IECLB

Apart from local synod and congregational publications, the IECLB has a national newspaper (*Jornal Evangélico Luterano*), a magazine (*Novo Olhar*), publishing houses and a few radio programs. Its Web site (**www.luteranos.com.br**) is becoming more and more relevant.

In 2000, the church's *Office for Communication Services* was closed and its duties reorganized. So IECLB communication is not uniform and the church is still developing a communication policy. Due to Brazil's size and its cultural and religious diversity, it is essential that communication be used to consolidate the unity of the church in its many different contexts. An example is the national 2008-2012 mission campaigns planned to span different media and appeal to as large an audience as possible under the theme "God's Mission – Our Passion."

The church practices *affirmative* communication that highlights good and positive points, and the dialogue has been improved. IECLB communication seeks to constantly increase the number of contacts and correspondents in local congregations.

New Century – New Challenges

The IECLB Missionary Action Plan states that every missionary action implies a communication action. So community-based as well as mass media communication should be part of missionary action strategies. Different publics require different communication strategies. While taking into account the important commitment of lay people in the congregations, it is nonetheless necessary to seek advice from professionals in the area of communication. A challenge at all levels is for investment in communication to be recognized in church budgets.[3]

According to the IECLB Missionary Action Plan, all forms of communication support should be promoted and serve the unity of the church. The church should "show its face" and try to implement what the Action Plan suggests, like:

- identify all the churches and ecclesiastical buildings with the IECLB logo;
- place clear and attractive signs with the IECLB logo, the place, days and times of congregational gatherings at strategic points in each neighborhood, city and metropolis;

---

[3] The IECLB Missionary Action Plan 2008-2012. English version: **www.luteranos.com.br/attachments/Documentos/pami_ingles.pdf**

- in order for a congregation/parish to be quickly identified as belonging to the IECLB in phone books, outdoors and public places, the suggestion is to place the initials IECLB before the specific name - for example: "IECLB - Evangelical Congregation of ...."[4]

The Lutheran Church in Brazil needs and seeks communication that develops the feeling of belonging, so that every member can be convinced that "I'm a part of this church." To increase its chances of achieving this objective, its communication should be inclusive and simple, based on a "bottom-up method" that sets a high value on people and offers feedback opportunities to its members.

A Short Illustration: The Transforming Dimension of Communication

A course on "The transforming dimension of communication" was an example of IECLB support to communication of and in its congregations according to a "bottom-up method." This weekend course was held three times in 2005 for nine out of the church's 18 synods in three different regions of southern Brazil. Unfortunately, available financial resources have not yet allowed the course to be held in other regions. A total of about 50 people, most of whom already had some practical knowledge in communication, participated in these courses, and all brought a lot of enthusiasm in achieving and sharing new skills. The course program mixed theory and praxis, and its challenge was to rediscover the importance of communication and build the capacity of participants so that they could create and use opportunities for communicating "who we are and what we believe in as IECLB."

> The training was conducted by a journalist and an assistant who ran a workshop. Guidelines were shared on how to write a journalistic text, and radio and photography workshops were also integrated. The participants were encouraged to be "correspondents" and to provide regular information about their congregations for publication in the church press or on its Web site, the aim being to create a network of "church communicators."

Summarizing his impressions, one participant testified that "It was a great experience. I learned how to see reality from a different angle. And I learned

---

[4] The IECLB Missionary Action Plan 2000-2007. English version: **www.luteranos.com.br**

to listen to what other synods have to say." The training was enabled through partnership with the Brazilian Union of Christian Communicators and organized by the National Council of Communication.

The IECLB needs urgently to continue to improve communication within its membership at all the different levels. As a creative and faithful church, it will find new ways to preach and to communicate the gospel in the Brazilian context—because the IECLB's passion is God's mission.

Europe

Communication at the Core of the Church or Church-related Organizations

Some considerations on KALME [1] and changing concepts of communication

Praxedis Bouwman

Communication is a complex symbolic process whereby reality is produced, maintained, repaired and transformed. Communication is intertwined with culture either, as some consider, leading it or, as others say, playing a dominant role. Even deeper, it is a basic human need and right, socially necessary for cohesion. That means its core is to make identity communicable. The last two statements are basics of communication in relation to religion (as is the culture component).

In the "new" thinking (and leaving the "old" thinking about communication as a process of transmission behind us), communication is a mutual effort to build community. Related to religion, it is a mutual effort to build a meaningful community. If we examine their documents on communication, we will discover that some European Lutheran churches are developing ways for communication to break new ground by discarding old habits. This "new" thinking is based on changing views on the importance of audiences. It is reconsidering the tensions between transmission, proclamation and dialogue. It is rethinking the whole process of communication and its relation with theology, including with the church itself.

In relation to the above, the decision taken over 30 years ago to name KALME as a "Communication Committee" was an excellent, and even startling choice considering the time that has passed since then. It is amazing how the choice of this name left the field open to developments in the discipline of communication even though at that time the concept of making churches visible was top down

---

[1] Communication Committee for Lutheran Minority Churches in Europe.

and based on the idea of transmission. What was very special about KALME right from the beginning was its vision of exchange, of including Eastern European churches during the era of the Iron Curtain and its efforts to somehow be this European communion of Lutheran small churches.

Developments within communication are visible in KALME's history, in how its concept has changed over time. Although KALME is still a means of supporting the public work of the churches in its modern expressions concentrated on (mass) media, it is also responsible for the development of the whole concept of communication, including a focus on audiences. Keeping audiences in mind, thinking of a more holistic approach to communication, locating communication at the same level in the organization as theology and mission, implies the need to think contextually. There is no one recipe that fits all churches. The way to shape communication depends on local/regional circumstances, on the society, on technical possibilities and much much more.

But having communication at the heart of a church organization definitely does not mean a huge communication department. Rather, it means that the whole organization is aware of the importance of communicating and of re-considering again and again what to communicate and how. Communication at the heart of the organization requires flexible professionals working in, for example, an octopus configuration. Or better, in the Lutheran context, in the shape of a Luther rose with each of the central church disciplines in the cross reaching out to the very tips (and preferably beyond) of the rose petals.

This is why KALME has become more flexible in providing assistance and expertise. Lutheran churches within KALME can benefit from participation in the network, irrespective of the stage of communication strategies/policies at which they find themselves.

KALME works in communication at two levels: practical and strategic. By organizing regular seminars and consultations, KALME also contributes to strengthening the LWF European minority churches in their communion.

On the practical side, KALME assists the churches with hands-on communication: how to produce news, articles, newsletters, magazines, radio and television programs and Internet material as well as how to deal with mass media.

On the strategic side, KALME is promoting a more holistic view of communication at the level of church leadership. As the participants of a KALME seminar on "Communication as strategy" in Piliscsaba in 2008 stated, communication should be right at the heart of the organization.

In the professional and ecumenical field of church and church-related communication, a division can be seen between thinking of communication as a service department that provides hands-on, communication products, and viewing it as holistic communication for the organization (as the LWF itself does by taking communication into its cabinet decision-making process). In these exciting post-Iron Curtain times, it is interesting to see the changes European churches are making. While eastern European churches try to catch up with a fast information society and, at the same time, rebuild churches out of the ruins of totalitarian regimes, western European churches face an increasingly secularizing society. Both sets of churches had to redefine their position, and are still doing so.

With this background, the above-mentioned seminar in Piliscsaba was a very exciting one, and had an amazingly unanimous outcome. Awareness that communication must be thoroughly professional is gaining ground. Communication in our complex societies cannot be reduced to public relations, and should not be confused with either marketing or fundraising. Integrating communication into the organizational decision-making process changes the decisions and makes organizations easily accessible and transparent—an essential requirement in today's "zapping" society.

From Information to Conversation, from Understanding to Trust

Communication in the Evangelical Lutheran Church of Latvia

Ivars Kupcis

It is commonly understood that communication is an integral component of the church's mission. The meaningful existence of the church in society is not possible without following its mission call given by Christ, just as this mission cannot be fulfilled without communication by Christ's followers with their surrounding communities, their neighbors. In this short summary, I will try to give some brief insights on the development of communication work in the Evangelical Lutheran Church of Latvia (ELCL).

Communication – An Integral Part of the Church's Existence

Latvia is one of the small but challenging countries on the Baltic Sea in northeastern Europe. One of our strengths is religious diversity, and particularly the strong traditions of the largest Christian denominations. Lutheran, Roman Catholic, Orthodox and Baptist churches have continued ecumenical cooperation, and the church has played an essential role in the most important turns in our nation's path to freedom and independence. The Evangelical Lutheran Church is one of the largest churches in Latvia, and it is usually considered as the national church in our country, although our legislation prescribes strict separation between church and state. When the country gained its independence in the 1990s, the church found itself in a free market of beliefs that made its communication efforts even more vital.

This paper will not deal with the communication activities that are part of the daily ministry of pastors and congregations, but focus on communication efforts of the church as an organization. For many years, the understandable public voice of the church was its archbishop. However, when church ministry areas were developed after 2000, the need for a communications institution—or at least a person—became evident. An institution or person needed to be aware of all the church's different activities and be responsible for communicating them to the appropriate audiences. So the ELCL Public Relations Commission was founded in 2005.

From Information to Conversation

The Public Relations Commission was established at the same organizational level as other commissions dealing with youth work, Sunday schools, education, diakonia, etc., to coordinate the church's communication activities. For the church, the most valuable benefit of its work was an increased possibility for dialogue with society and media, as well as a significant improvement of internal communication. If church communication before that could be measured as a mainly one-way information flow to its audience, so now the church was able to enter into conversation with its audiences to a greater extent, connecting with internal as well as external publics. It became possible not only to answer questions raised by the media, but also to provide the media with topics deemed important by the church.

From the start, the PR Commission's main tasks included media relations, internal communication activities, producing printed materials, coordinating the church newspaper, as well as development of the new ELCL Web site.

Understanding Leads to Trust – Inside and Outside

In the 2007 ELCL Communications Plan, the main goal of the church's public relations work was defined as that of **building trust toward the church in society and increasing mutual understanding within the church**, its members and all institutional levels.

ELCL communication activities still go in two directions: church communication with society, and internal communication. According to the current definition of ELCL communication tasks, the goals of church communication with society are:

- to maintain the church's reputation in order to help it to carry out its mission;
- to provide information about church activities;
- to express the church's views on important social, ethical and other issues.

The church has also identified the main target publics of its communication:

- Lutherans (that is, roughly a quarter of Latvia's population, who consider themselves as belonging to the Lutheran tradition although most of them have no active connection with any local congregation);
- society in general;
- the media.

At the same time, the goals for internal communication are:

- to maintain effective communication within the church, parishes and among parishioners on important issues for the church;
- to assist in building mutual understanding about the mission of the church;
- to raise awareness of Lutheran tradition and Lutheran identity within the church.

And the main target audiences for internal communication are:

- parish members;
- parish leaders;
- pastors;
- the church Council, its members and employees.

However, distinct boundaries can no longer be drawn between the church's inside and outside audiences. For example, many journalists are church members. On the one hand, this is an advantage for the church. On the other, it also challenges them to be honest to both their church and their employers. At the same time, a lot of church members, and even more those Lutherans who are not strongly connected to any local parish, use the secular media to get news about the church and its activities. This situation is just one more reason why the church needs to communicate openly and honestly with all publics, whether they are church members or not. Better understanding of the church and its role thus leads to increased trust, which can greatly help the church to carry out its mission.

Toward Fruitful Cooperation between Church and Media

One of the ELCL PR Commission's main activity areas is media relations, enabling better understanding and cooperation between the church and the media. From time to time, news agencies, press, TV, radio and internet news media focus on the church. Quite frequently however, topics that raise media interest in the church are not quite the same as those that the church itself would select as a first priority for communication. Mutual understanding between the church and the media on their respective roles cannot be built in a day, but is part of an ongoing process of improvement.

Media relations in the ELCL started professionally with the appointment of professional staff in 2005. The dissemination of church news releases as well as preparing information on church issues when requested by journalists still plays an important role. Crisis communication in the case of conflict situations or misunderstandings connected with the church or its activities is also a less frequent but quite significant task. This usually relates to church real estate that has not yet been fully returned by the state or, when it has been returned, sometimes unfortunately raises misunderstandings.

So whether the issue at hand is primarily important for church mission or whether it responds to short-term media interest, our task is to provide the church's opinion to the media and to present it in the best way possible. As a result, about 300 articles on issues related to our church were published in the Latvian press in 2008. Of course, not all the articles were entirely positive, but almost 90 percent presented the opinion of the church and ensured that it was heard by the general public.

Newspaper – Traditional but Still Popular

One traditional and historically experienced communication channel of our church is the *Svētdienas Rīts* (Sunday Morning) newspaper. Started in 1920, it operated in the beginning as the mission newsletter of the Lutheran Church, and then became the official newspaper of the Latvian Evangelical Lutheran Church. Shut down by Soviet occupation in the 1940s, it was re-established right after the fall of the regime as Latvia gained its independence and oppression of the church ended.

Currently, the paper contributes to internal communication between church members, and serves the needs of audiences with a special interest in ELCL activities. At the moment, its target audience is the 42,000 active members of ELCL parishes. At the same time, it could strive to reach a much wider audience of 400-600,000 Lutheran tradition-related people in general, but that is still a fairly distant, although desired, goal. Thus the paper's main aim at present is to establish mutually beneficial relations between individual members of parishes and the church in general.

One of the questions the newspaper will need to answer in the context of over-all future church communication strategy will be related to the future concept of *Svētdienas Rīts*. The church will need to decide whether to maintain its newspaper as an official ELCL organ focusing mostly on church events and local parishes, or to meet the current communication needs of Lutherans, or even Christians in general, covering a wider range of events and processes within our society.

A more practical issue related to the newspaper's future is the possibility of developing a Web version. Although the ELCL official Web site now provides news about church activities, a separate Internet news portal would allow a lot more effective communication, reaching a larger audience and providing opportunities for user-generated content as well.

ELCL Web Site – A Dynamic News Source

Thus the Lutheran Church's most dynamic communication channel is now its Web site, **www.lelb.lv**. With its quite extensive and structured information on church ministry areas, congregations, pastors and institutions, the site serves as a comprehensive source of information on the Lutheran Church and its ministry. A daily updated news section helps church members and other interested visitors to keep up with current events in the church. A subscription service allows subscribers to be among the first to receive news from the church's authorized news source.

Members of ELCL parishes as well as those who are searching for spirituality and their way to God and the church constitute the Web site's target audience. An English version although less extensive serves the information needs of churches and individuals abroad, providing basic information about our church.

The goal of the Web site is to provide news and information about the church and its activities, as well as to receive feedback from target groups. According to the statistics, almost every second active church member visits the site at least once a month. While there is room for growth, this coverage is quite an encouraging achievement since not all church members are active Internet users.

One of the site's most visited pages is a discussion forum open to everyone. It hosts often rather harsh discussions on various topics related to Christian belief, important church issues as well as many controversial questions. Moderated by a few volunteers, the forum usually attracts the interest of those who are already church members. The question as to what impression this makes on visitors who are maybe contacting the church for the first time is often raised. The benefits from good theological discussions and critical conversations on important church issues sometimes seem to be outweighed by inappropriate user behavior enabled by the anonymous nature of the Internet.

It would seem that in regard to the further development of the ELCL Web site, we will need to make a choice. The first and most understandable option is to build it as a mission-oriented tool for church ministry, meeting the needs of searching individuals. The second option is to create a news and discussion portal for church members whose more sophisticated needs for insight in specific areas of church ministry would be of little interest to first-time visitors. Even if the decision were made to combine these two options in one site, as is more or less the case at present, the main needs of searchers and newcomers—including information on baptism, confirmation, pastoral care, etc.—should then already be addressed on the front page.

From Public Relations to Mission?

If we understand the main mission of the church to be to lead people into a close relationship with God through his son Jesus Christ, so the task of church communication cannot be much different. Church communication does everything in its power to help the church in its mission. Thus communication itself becomes part of the mission.

The archbishop of the Evangelical Lutheran Church of Latvia, Janis Vanags, once said that our church needs public relations only insofar as it helps to carry out the church's mission to preach the gospel. This was true before the PR Commission was founded, and it is even truer now, five years later.

Looking at the potential further development of communication in the Evangelical Lutheran Church of Latvia, the direction we need to take therefore seems quite clear: we need to move from public relations to mission.

North America

Mission and Ministry of the Churches' Work

Communication in the Evangelical Lutheran Church in Canada

Trina Gallop

The landscape of communication within the Evangelical Lutheran Church in Canada (ELCIC), along with the landscape of communication in general, has changed significantly over the past five years.

While the introduction of new technologies is happening at ever-increasing speed, one thing continues to remain the same. As reported by the Communication Review Task Force in its 2004 report to the ELCIC National Church Council (NCC), "the ELCIC has the greatest potential to live out its mission statement when all three of its expressions—national, synod and congregations—work in concert. While all three have unique functions, a basic and important national responsibility is communication. Communication unites the church and builds relationships that strengthen faith and ministries."

Recognizing that communication is central to the ELCIC's vision and strategic directions, the NCC asked its national bishop to appoint a Communication Review Task Force. In March 2005, the NCC heard both the findings from the intensive review of the Task Force, which affirmed many of the communication practices that were in place at the time, and received the recommendations of a two-year Communications Task Force Study, which set out a number of priorities for the church, including:

- hiring a communications director (previously no one individual was solely tasked with this responsibility);
- maintaining the ELCIC's national publication, *Canada Lutheran*, but enhancing its connection to the national office;
- broadening the communication strategy to engage a wider audience;

- improving ecumenical communication partnerships to maximize shared resources and develop a "presence in Canadian society."

The following is an overview of a few key areas within the current ELCIC communications strategy.

Branding and Visual Identity

The Communications Review Task Force identified the need to "ensure a common look for all communication materials and resources." One of the first strategies introduced was a branding and visual identity strategy; which also led the way forward for many other areas of the communication strategy. Branding brought consistency to the work and lifted up priorities of the church. Most significantly, branding identified that we are a church *in mission for others*. This call to mission is so important that we use the language deliberately, even identifying it in our redesigned logo.

Web Site

The ELCIC undertook a redesign of the Web site, one of our most significant communication tools, in 2007. This strategy was embarked on to bring it in line with the branding strategy, but also to reorganize the information to make it more user-friendly and ensure that the users of the site could find what they were looking for… and engage them in new areas of ministry that perhaps they were interested in but didn't even know the ELCIC was involved in. Currently, within the ELCIC communication strategy, we are investigating opportunities to engage new communication media into our mix including the use of tools such as Facebook and Twitter to broaden our reach and engage a wider audience. While understanding that these tools have the potential to engage a wider audience, it also means doing communication differently. Web 2.0 means that communication is no longer just about putting information outward, but that it is also about receiving information through these communication media as well and engaging in ongoing dialogue with our constituency.

Media

The ELCIC communication strategy calls for proactive work in seeking out opportunities for storytelling through the media. This has become somewhat more difficult as many secular publications across Canada have faced a number of challenges as communication media change and new technologies take the place of print-based publications. In Canada, we note that fewer publications are devoting time and resources to faith stories and features. Recognizing that coverage can provide both awareness-building opportunities and credibility (both to our members and beyond the church walls), relationship-building with key writers and faith journalists is a key part of the strategy.

Canada Lutheran

The ELCIC's national publication, *Canada Lutheran*, is published eight times a year and seeks to inspire and engage the members of the church in connecting faith to everyday life. As a print publication, the magazine has its challenges and is faced with continually increasing costs for production. We are monitoring these and continue to investigate enhancing the publication with a stronger online presence although we don't have the resources to do that at this time.

Utilizing Effective Partnerships

One of the ELCIC's five areas of focus, effective partnerships, calls the ELCIC to not do alone what we could do in partnership. This is good stewardship of resources but it is also a current reality in which we live. In many areas of communication, partnership is sought internally and with other denominations and organizations to expand our breadth and abilities. Through a staff secondment arrangement, two communication staff members from the Anglican Church of Canada (ACC)—with which the ELCIC is in full communion—assisted with the communication efforts of the 2009 ELCIC National Convention. These individuals shared their gifts and talents to assist us in our communication work for the convention so that we could take on a greater capacity and do more than we would have been able to do without them. In return, a staff member from the ELCIC communication department will assist on the communication team for the ACC's General

Synod in 2010. We also try to identify opportunities with the Evangelical
Lutheran Church in America's (ELCA) communication department for col-
laborating where we work jointly, and with other agencies such as Canadian
Lutheran World Relief—sharing the work around telling the stories of our
church in mission for others.

While the landscape of communication within the ELCIC and in general
continues to change at an ever-increasing pace, new technologies present us
with new opportunities. Through all of this, the ELCIC's communication
strategy seeks:

1. Awareness and Involvement
   - ensuring that ELCIC members are aware of the mission and min-
     istry of the church;
   - access to available resources for involvement in ministry and leader-
     ship.

2. Public voice
   - The ELCIC speaks out clearly to its members, the public forum
     and the international community.

3. The ELCIC communicates our Lutheran identity to and with interchurch
   and interfaith communities.

Ecumenical News International

Communication – Our Daily Bread

Peter Kenny

I work as editor-in-chief of *Ecumenical News International*—a news agency that covers news of every facet of the Church and its intersection with other religions from all corners of the globe. We distribute our news to all branches of secular and church media via e-mail, print and the Internet. We also supply our news to institutions and individuals in the hopes of facilitating the service and development of humanity and enabling an essential discourse.

Since we cover all churches, we are ecumenical—according to the vision of our founding members—the World Council of Churches, the Lutheran World Federation, the World Alliance of Reformed Churches and the Conference of European Churches.

The groups which support *ENI* are amalgams of churches, some of them communions—all rooted in the ecumenical ideal of a united church. That is why they support *ENI* as a news agency, an ecumenical news agency that carries news about their member churches, their non-member churches and other faiths. If the essence of being ecumenical is being inclusive, that is how we try to present the church via *ENI*.

The Good News and the Bad News

From the perspective of both the secular and the church world, the Bible is often referred to in English as the "Good News." Its contents, however, do not appear to be just an unexpurgated litany of "good news" but a complex series of real life dramas, plots, intrigues and complex relations that unfurl the path to the good news. And insofar as the New Testament in the Bible is concerned, there is one recurring theme. It has one man—the Son of God—our Saviour Jesus—talking truth to power. In the Bible, in order to get to the part that has the good news, you have also to read about sectors that sometimes have what could appear to be some tracts of rather bad or unsettling news.

Having said that, as you will have rightly surmised by now, I am not a theologian. I am a journalist. Some people call this one of the world's oldest professions, based on the tool of communications. As soon as one imparts information about anything to another human being, one is communicating; and we all know the biblical reference to the beginning starting with the "word." Our pastoral adviser Theo Gill alluded to this so eloquently in his prayers earlier.

Since human beings first thumped out drum beats from hill to hill to tell their neighbors about upcoming events, we have been communicating. Journalism has evolved as a form of factual storytelling for human beings to inform humanity about what goes on.

Some people are surprised when they learn that journalism is neither an ideology nor a religion, and not a political party. It is merely a tool for communicating in true story format the day-to-day occurrences in life. It has a similarity to the Bible in that journalism at its best is speaking truth to power through storytelling. This is especially so when it is doing so on behalf of a person or entity that has not, until the delivery of the piece of journalism, been empowered to do so.

Old Technology – Perennial Stories

When I worked in one of my first newspaper bureaus in an area of South Africa then called the Transkei during an era under the odious system of apartheid, I would punch my stories out on a piece of ticker tape and send them to my newspaper via a telex machine. The photographer who worked with me would process photographs in a darkroom using complicated light machines and smelly chemicals. Then the photographer would roll the photographs onto a drum which made a squealing noise for 30 minutes for each black and white photograph sent to our newspaper editor, the late Donald Woods. He was a man of deep faith who had to flee his country because he exposed a truth about a man called Steve Biko. Sometimes we would send out stories and pictures that we had both got beaten for; or we might have spent some pointless sojourn in police custody for acquiring them.

Church leaders such as Desmond Tutu, Allan Boesak, Beyers Naudé and Desmond Hurley led an ecumenical challenge in South Africa when it was most needed, providing the dough for the daily bread of countless journalists to let the world know some very unpalatable truths about what was really going on in that country.

At the time, in the 1970s and 1980s, when I and my colleagues were slogging away with our attempts to tell a story that many of my own people and our government did not want told, ecumenical gatherings, particularly assemblies of the World Council of Churches in Uppsala and Vancouver, were discussing the relationship of theology to mass communication. According to the published *History of the Ecumenical Movement*:

> "There was a recognition of the inadequacy of any one means of communication—pulpit-press-broadcasting, the institutional church or the spoken and unspoken witness of the individual Christian—to carry the whole burden of God's revelation of himself." At the Uppsala assembly of the WCC, a statement was adopted called, "The Church and the Media of Mass Communication."

The statement adopted in Uppsala defended the variety of media as enriching human life and culture. At the same time, the media were seen as tools through which to promote the cornerstones of a responsible world society. Further, the media were seen to provide a forum for discussing the crucial issues of the time and to give minority views a public hearing.

Those churches at Uppsala were therefore placing the media on the agenda of the ecumenical movement. Throughout the 1970s, the issue of communication was dealt with in a still wider context. When debate over the WCC's Programme to Combat Racism arose, the ecumenical movement had to learn the operations of the mass media, especially when opponents challenged it for supporting liberation movements that at the time were labelled "terrorist groups" by some. Ecumenical groups advocating justice in ways controversial to some of their own church members had to learn to communicate effectively.

Smartphones and Netbooks

Now in the 21st century, the same dictum applies. Instead of the drums of our forebears, and the landline drums of my generation, we have smartphones, netbooks, notebooks and satellite dishes that send and receive our messages and news. The SMS is the new telegram.

Throughout its history, Christianity has been connected to both the material developments of the printed word and the essence of all credible journalism—the telling of a truth to humanity. Journalism is often based on our belief in the righteousness of truth, and it is always linked to facts. Those of us who have an ounce of sense in our heads know that those who say science and religion can't coexist are both ungodly and unscientific.

And we all know what explosive advances took place regarding the mass media in the 20th century. I have alluded briefly to some of them.

To return to our theme here—give us this day our daily bread.

For *ENI*, the news of the church is our daily bread as it reveals the life of this body in its totality. The tools may have changed since the 1970s and '80s, but churches must continue to serve those in their midst and outside, in the name of God. We serve the church by making it our mission to elucidate on how it does, or does not, serve.

Journalists have to continue using the tools of narrative and storytelling through words, pictures and sound.

Journalists of my ilk look outwards to the secular world and inwards at the church, and attempt to explain how they intersect and function, through all their glories and foibles. It is joyous and painful, just like life.

So I ask those of you who are, and who will be, theologians not to give up in mapping out ways of examining what is the right path for both of us—so we can continue to provide the daily bread upon which we all depend—news stories and analyses about the life of the Church in its entirety.

Reflections on Communication from Morning and Evening Prayer

Theodore Gill

Wednesday 17 June 2009

"Loaves abound!" – Opening communion: Matthew 6:5-15

In the beginning was the Word.

In Hebrew scripture, the Word sounds as a divine command, an irresistible invocation to being and becoming. It begins with the forceful phrase, "Let there be…"

Let there be light. Let there be a space for life. Let there be sun and moon and stars. Let there be earth and plants and animals. And finally, "Let us make humanity in our own image." All of this is accomplished through "the Word." The act of creation is simultaneously an act of communication.

"And the Word became flesh." The act of redemption is simultaneously the coming of God's Word among us, taking its place in our midst.

And at Pentecost, the realization of the Spirit moving through the nascent church is simultaneously a vision of "tongues" descending from heaven, tongues with which believers may utter comprehensible, communicative words concerning the Word.

Our theme this week, as at next year's LWF assembly in Stuttgart, is "Our Daily Bread." What is the connection between "the Word of God" and "our daily bread"? Perhaps there is a hint in the prophetic rebuke of Isaiah 55:2, "Why do you spend your money on that which is not bread?" We suspect, too, that it has to do with the elements of communion on this table before us, and with the table-fellowship to which we are invited.

This morning, a number of us visited the offices of Mission EineWelt in Neuendettelsau, a center of Lutheran service, and there one member of the staff told us, "Mission Einewelt brings people to a table. Not just to the Lord's table, although that is part of it. Ours is a ministry of outreach, mission and diakonia that aims to feed the body and the soul." It is a ministry that deals in both bread and Word.

And now we find ourselves at a table in the chapel of the Martin Luther Bund. This room is also a part of the Martin Luther Bund's library, and so we find ourselves gathered at a table that stands literally beneath the cross, yet also over against a high wall of shelves crammed with works of theology. From the look of the books, some get more use than others. Many tomes have gathered layers of dust despite once having communicated the gospel to generations of students who became well-educated pastors in the church.

But as we look at that wall of books, we must wonder whether these are the tools of communication best suited to our context. On our drive back from Neuendettelsau, our coach passed under a gigantic broadcast tower that dominates the landscape around Nuremburg. Perhaps we could have paused and paid a visit: the chances are that such an imposing electronic facility has something to teach us about communicating that is not contained in these aging volumes. Ideas in the books are well worth considering; however, their voices are not heard as clearly today as when they first appeared.

Yesterday when I came out of the Erlangen rail station I found myself at the corner of Goethestrasse and Calvinstrasse. Since I am a minister of the Reformed tradition living in Geneva during this year of "Calvin 500" anniversary celebrations, "Calvinstrasse" made me feel right at home. "Goethestrasse," of course, reminded me of language courses at school and university—the study of folk ballads and poetic revisions of them by the likes of Goethe and Heine—and eventually this reminded me of a story told in my family...

My mother's father was the son of German immigrants who lived in a market town in the US state of Iowa. According to the collective family memory, almost all the residents of that small town were German-Americans. But near the end of the 19th century, animosity intensified between the Catholic German-Americans and the Protestant German-Americans. As an expression of their enmity, the Catholics took to speaking among themselves only in German, while the Protestants began to use English exclusively. The result was that my grandfather's brothers and sisters remembered a little German, having been older when Protestants made the switch to English, but their younger brother knew almost nothing of his ancestral language.

In later life, my grandfather told my mother that there was only one phrase of German that he could recall. He believed it was something his mother had said to him—or possibly sung to him—when he was very small. These are the German words:

Ich weiss nicht, was soll es bedeuten…

"I don't know what it means," he said to my mother (which, ironically, is precisely what the phrase means: "I don't know what it can mean…" It could be a comic dialogue: "'Ich weiss nicht, was soll es bedeuten': I don't know what it means!" – "Exactly!!")

My grandfather's story remained on my mother's mind, German words and all, even though she never studied that language in school. It was only when I took German classes, decades after my grandfather's death, that I ran across the folk tradition of the "Lorelei," river sirens who lured sailors to their doom, a folk legend recorded by Goethe and turned into a popular song by Heinrich Heine and Friedrich Silcher. It was the out-of-context opening line of that song which haunted my grandfather through the years.

Today, I look at the dusty books ranked opposite the communion table, and I think of my grandfather puzzling over those half-forgotten words, telling himself, "I don't know what it means." And I think of the dust that covers Bibles in so many homes within our cultures, and the teachings that lie half-forgotten in them as their owners grope for meaning in their lives.

And I think, too, of words to a communion hymn by Fred Kaan, set to a Jamaican calypso melody by the late Doreen Potter:

> Let us talents and tongues employ, reaching out with a shout of joy:
> bread is broken, the wine is poured, Christ is spoken and seen and heard.
> Jesus lives again, earth can breathe again. Pass the Word around:
> Loaves abound!

Evening prayer: Deuteronomy 8:3, Matthew 4:1-4

> One does not live by bread alone, but by every word that comes from the mouth of God.

Not *every* word proceeds from the mouth of God; even words of Holy Scripture may be twisted to demonic uses, to Satanic uses. "Come along," Satan entices, "throw yourself from this height—for *it is written* that God will give the angels charge over you, and they will not let you be bruised." In the present instance, though, Satan employs logic rather than proof-texts: (1) God gives you power to turn stones to bread; (2) You are hungry, and surrounded by stones; (3) Therefore… ? It is a straightforward syllogism.

But Jesus rejects this word, this logic, because he knows the speaker. He is fasting as a means of seeking a word that comes from the mouth of God;

nothing less will do. Satan's argument shows sophistication in its logic, a feigned respect in its appreciation of what Jesus is able to do. "Take the bread you need. Put your talent to work. Use the raw material at hand."

Jesus is looking for something even more basic than bread. At first glance, fasting may seem contradictory to the prayer for daily bread, but this is what one of our speakers has cited as "constructive contradiction." In his commitment to fasting and his quest for the proper word, Jesus doubts Satan's concern for human well-being. He finds the devil's advice to be anything *but* "credible communication."

This is still a very early moment in our consultation, but the text on Christ's temptation in the wilderness may suggest one provisional conclusion: words and other vehicles of communication are not valuable in themselves. Even Satan can quote the Bible. Not just any "bread" will do, no matter how hungry we are. There may be a case for "art for art's sake," but: *No* to communion for communion's sake alone. *No* to communication for communication's sake.

The value of communication is no mere matter of reason or sophistication, nor of utilizing particular systems and processes in disseminating a message. More important is the heart of the messenger and the consequence of the words.

Thursday 18 June 2009

Morning prayer: Ecclesiastes 11:1-6, Luke 8:4-15

> Cast your bread upon the waters… Plant your seeds in the morning…

When my daughter was young, we used to cast bread upon the waters fairly often. We called it "feeding the ducks." The phrase in Ecclesiastes is not crystal-clear in meaning, and has been liable to numerous interpretations. A search on the Internet indicates that many optimistic believers these days feel it offers practical advice on investments in global markets having to do with diversification and international opportunities. My guess is that we do well to seek alternate exegetical understandings.

It seems to me that one consistent teaching in Holy Scripture is that "the waters" are under God's control. God alone is master of them. In the beginning it was God who separated waters from waters to create a space for life. Noah escaped destruction in the waters of the flood because of a timely word from God. At the Exodus, the waters of the Red Sea were parted, just as the waters of Jordan ceased to flow 40 years later and piled up in a heap while the people of God entered the land of promise. The most mysterious depths, the waters of the Great Sea, obeyed the command of God in the days of Jonah, those vast expanses which God had offered as the home and playground of Leviathan.

To the people of the Hebrew kingdoms, "the waters" were strange, foreign, the embodiment of other-worldliness. And this is what makes that suggestion so striking, "Cast your bread upon the waters…" The original readers knew that they could have no control over what would happen if they committed their goods, their lives, their hopes to the unpredictable waves. Yet God commands: Do not be afraid of the unfamiliar. Do not hesitate to entrust your future to God.

It is a sort of parable, an allegory, this metaphorical treatment of bread and waters. Later, Jesus taught his disciples in parables—Jesus, who once stilled a storm at sea so that his disciples asked one another, "Who is this that even the wind and waves obey?"

In the parable of Jesus we read this morning, a man sets out to plant seeds by flinging them far and wide from the sack of seeds tied at his waist—he *casts* them *broadly*, and this is the original meaning of the English word "*broadcasting*." The trouble with such a profligate approach to sowing is that some of the seed is bound to fall on ground where it is unlikely to flourish. But the message of Jesus is *not*, "Stop using this inefficient method of planting!" The parable simply reminds disciples that outcomes are not within our control, yet *some* seeds take root and grow and bring forth grain a hundredfold.

Cast your bread upon the waters; plant your seeds in the morning; broadcast the Word throughout the world. And then, trust God to shape creation, even within clouds of mystery, even when *we* do not understand what is happening.

Evening prayer: Luke 24:28-35

> Then they told what had happened on the road, and how he had been made known to them in the breaking of the bread.

We have heard a good deal today about hermeneutics, and we learn even more from Luke's account of the conversation on the way to Emmaus and the report of it afterwards.

The disciples did not recognize the stranger on the road—any more than Mary Magdalene recognized the "gardener" as Jesus, in John's resurrection narrative, until the Lord called her by name. The stranger on the road upbraided the disciples for their lack of comprehension and "foolishness" as they discussed the events of recent days. We don't know how they felt about that exchange at the time, but in retrospect—after the breaking of the bread in Emmaus—they appreciated all that had passed between them.

All our talk of hermeneutics, of the difficulties that arise in trying to communicate across cultures, can be discouraging when taken in large doses—as we have decidedly been dosing ourselves today. One even begins to wonder if true "communication" is possible! As part of this evening's reflection, I would like to share a passage from a book called *Interpreting Disability: A Church of All and for All* [WCC Publications, 2004]. It is a book about ideas, policies and practices within the church regarding the relationship between people with disabilities and those who are not generally considered "disabled." Arne Fritzson, one of the authors, introduces himself in a way that I hope may aid us in thinking about the application of hermeneutics in communicating:

> To write a book is a pretentious thing. It is to make a claim to have a story to tell. This book is about the concerns of people with disabilities, and it is about the Christian faith. Why should I, of all persons, tell you something about these things?
>
> I am a person with a disability, cerebral palsy, and I am a Christian, an ordained pastor in a small, reformed Swedish free church—the Mission Covenant Church of Sweden. I am also a male, married, Western, academically trained, white person with a middle-class background. I belong to that tradition that for too long a time has claimed to do basic *theology* while others are doing special forms of *theologies*. And there are a lot of Christians who live with different forms of disabilities. So why should I, of all people, write about disability and Christian faith? Now, when the World Council of Churches provides a space for this important conversation, why should I occupy that space? I, who belong to a culture of colonizers, even though my country had a very small part in the history of European colonization? Am I too a colonizer when I claim this arena to put forward my thoughts on this important subject? Are there not more important voices to be heard? Voices that for too long were silenced, people whose stories need to be told and heard?
>
> This could be interpreted as an overly defensive, self-justifying way to start a book. But that is not my intention. I do believe that there are complications impeding my project of writing a book. Nonetheless, I am writing. After all, whoever might have written this book could be accused of colonizing this space; so why not me, in spite of my background? I never chose to belong to a category that has been privileged at others' expense, even though history may have had it that way. So why not take this opportunity to express my views and do it with vigour and pride, and pretend that all the problems I have mentioned do not exist, even though I know that they are real and pressing? A lot of people choose to handle these problems of interpretation by ignoring them, seemingly as a way of giving up the possibility of handling them in other and more cautious ways...

I do not believe there is a way to transcend the particularity of an author's experience. But I do believe that there is a more fruitful way to handle it than just to ignore it. In fact this is what the current text is all about. It is written out of the conviction that the fact that we all have different stories creates a gap between us that we never fully bridge. Our bodily constitutions make it impossible for us fully to understand life from another human being's perspective. We literally cannot walk in others' shoes; even so, it is possible for us to share fragments of understanding and at least partially to grasp others' experiences of what it is to live as a human being in God's world.

We can share fragments, nothing more, nothing less. This means that an expression will have a different meaning for you than it has for me. We cannot fully understand each other, at least if we try to discuss existential questions. Consequently, we should have an attitude that is both critical and generous, both humble and proud, both in writing and reading. It must be generous and humble so we respect the one with whom we are communicating, and critical and proud so we dare to communicate what is important to us and critically discern what we receive, not accepting everything we are told.

I am raising a hermeneutical question, a question about interpretation, and this is natural for someone like me who has a special interest in hermeneutics. Academic discourse has rightly been criticized for often being too insensitive to different contexts and claiming to speak about one universal human experience. While I try to do what I can to avoid that mistake here, this academic discourse is part of my context and as such I will use it as a resource for my thinking… (pp.1-2)

When the disciples returned from Emmaus, they made their report to those who had not been there. And another report of the risen Lord was offered on behalf of Simon. In this way the disciples compiled a base of knowledge, building a common wisdom, preparing to carry their personal experiences and shared faith in mission to the world.

Friday 19 June 2009

Morning prayer: Matthew 14:15-21

We have nothing here but five loaves and two fish…

It is a story of scarcity and abundance. Five loaves at the start, but twelve basketsful of bread left over.

The disciples knew how to *count*, so their focus was on the lack of budget for the project. Jesus knew how to *give*, so he said, "Put the loaves and fish into *my* hands."

As in the Emmaus account of Luke 24, the language of distribution is eucharistic: Jesus took this resource, he prayed, he blessed, he broke, he gave… and all who wished to share in the feast were fed.

There are several ideas about the Lord's Supper that we learned yesterday morning in the lectures on communication and hermeneutics in Christian history. For example, there is the concept of the Eucharist as a "journalistic genre"—telling the story and offering a form of the face-to-face communication that is our most effective means of imparting a message.

And, related to that idea, we also heard an intriguing reference to Hörisch's argument that the Christian Eucharist was one of the earliest means of mass communication—as significant in its way as the invention of standardized units of money or, much later, the birth of the Internet. Thus, the acts of dispersing and receiving the elements of communion may be regarded as meeting the highest standard of communication, revealing a significant truth to the audience and leading them to invest themselves in life.

The presence of Christ; the promise of the kingdom: these are resources offered in abundance by the one who called humanity to a more abundant life. But we, his followers, know only too well how to count, and our focus strays to line-items in the budget. We come to believe in the scarcity of resources available to us—there are not enough loaves, not enough fish, not enough euros.

"Come, now," says Jesus. "Put all that into *my* hands."

Jesus takes the available resources, blesses and divides them wisely. And he gives in abundance, so that there is more than enough for all.

Evening prayer: Mark 14:16-25

> It is one of the twelve, one who is dipping bread into the bowl with me.

Jesus and the disciples gather at table in an upper room: it is the archetype of our communion as Christians. Here we find Mark's account of the breaking and distribution of bread, yet here too we find the prophecy of betrayal: the traitor will be "one who is dipping bread in the bowl with me."

Even in this primal and optimal act of communion there is tension. One of the twelve will choose to communicate essential information to the agents of brutal control, violent repression and death.

To the disciples' credit, their first reaction to Jesus' warning is *not*, "Oh, you must be talking about **Judas**. I never liked him, anyway."

No. Each of the disciples responds, one after another, "Is it I, Lord?"

They admit in their hearts, "Someone is going to bring tragedy upon us all, and hand over our Lord to his enemies. And that traitor… Is it I? I cannot be entirely sure."

It is impossible to know what was in the mind of Judas Iscariot, although there have been attempts to explain his thinking—from the Gnostic *Gospel of Judas* in the second century to the rock-opera *Jesus Christ Superstar* just a generation or two ago. The common dynamic in these two portrayals of Judas is the claim that he was trying to *do Jesus a favor*, to pressure him in such a way that he would reveal himself there and then, either as the Savior transcending space and time or perhaps as a more worldly revolutionary leader inspiring the masses to rise up against Empire. In either case, it is argued, Judas was acting with the best of intentions. He intended to use the moment in such a way that people would be confronted by Christ and *forced* to accept the gospel.

Whatever was in Judas' mind, his communication of what he had learned from Jesus is remembered today as a gross betrayal of the message he had been called to bear. But was Judas' confusion and misunderstanding of his calling really *so* very different from some of the comments we hear in the gospels from the lips of Peter, or James and John, or Thomas? The action of Judas may have been fatal, but the difference in thinking behind his action varied from other apostles' thoughts only by subtle degrees.

And so the troubled, self-reflective question arises: "Is it I, Lord?" Will I—will *we*—deny or betray you, in word or in deed? Even with the best of intentions, will we fail you? There is no guarantee in sharing bread with Jesus, for even Judas did the same.

The responsibility we are given as Christian communicators is one to be undertaken with fear and trembling. Temptations will come our way, and the biblical question is still relevant: "Is it I, Lord?"

The ancient prayer, too, is as relevant as ever:

> Lord, have mercy. Christ, have mercy.
> Lord, have mercy, and grant us peace.

Saturday 20 June 2009

Morning prayer: John 6:30–40

> I am the bread of life.

The Lord is gracious and merciful. The Lord allows for our weakness. And so we trust God to supply "our daily bread."

Jesus says, "I am the bread of life," and in this discourse he draws a parallel between the grace he offers humanity and the gift of manna in the time of exodus, the bread from heaven given on a daily basis to a hard-pressed people. This manna was not to be hoarded but gathered fresh each day, with a double portion served up on the eve of Sabbath. The bread from heaven, the bread of life, is *daily bread*, spread before us for the taking.

In the written text of Brenda's [Akpan] presentation yesterday, there is a quotation from William Fore's 1987 book *Television and Religion: The Shaping of Faith, Values and Culture* [Augsburg Press, USA]. Bill Fore had a long and rich career as a professional communicator and as a consultant to a variety of churches and especially to the national council of churches in the United States. He offered strong opinions on the churches and their communication strategies, and you may agree or disagree with things he said; I offer two brief passages from his book for your consideration:

> …the purpose of Christian communication is *not* to ask, "How can we communicate the gospel in such a way that others will accept it?" This is the *wrong* question, the public relations question, the manipulative question, the question asked by the electronic church. Rather, our task is to put the gospel before people in such a way that it is so clear to them that they can accept it, or reject it—*but always for the right reasons*. As Tillich points out, it is better that people reject the gospel for the *right* reasons than that they accept it for the *wrong* reasons.
>
> Of course, one can never know with certainty what are the exactly "right" and "wrong" reasons for someone else, any more than we can know perfectly the innermost thought of others. Therefore, in fashioning our strategy of communication about the faith we can only act in faith, never in certainty. But our objective should always be to present the gospel in ways so clear and self-evident that the recipient will have an "Aha!" experience, so that the good news will make complete sense to his or her own inner world… (p.49)

> …for Christians the aim of communication is to help people interpret their existence in the light of what God has done for them as manifest in Jesus Christ. (p.48f.)

Helping people interpret their own experience… *not* trying to interpret it for them from afar. Describing what God has done, what God is doing, the meaning of God's abiding promise… a description of the bread from heaven that is offered to all, expressed with such clarity that the audience will exclaim, "Aha!" This is our task.

D.T. Niles famously remarked that Christian mission is like "one beggar telling another beggar where to find bread." And we know where our daily bread is to be found. Jesus says, "I am the bread of life. Whoever comes to me will never hunger, and whoever believes in me will never thirst."

"Lord," they said to him, "give us this bread always!"

Closing prayer: 1 Corinthians 10:16-17, Didache 1,9

> Blessed are those who hunger and thirst for righteousness, for they shall be satisfied.

Our second reading, complementing the one from 1 Corinthians, is a second-century eucharistic prayer recorded in the *Didache*:

> As this bread, once spread as wheat upon the hillsides,
> was brought into one loaf, so may your church
> be brought from the ends of the earth into your kingdom.

During an earlier service of worship we sang a lyric by Fred Kaan in which he prays to God, asking intercession "for those who hunger for acceptance, for righteousness and bread." In our Bible readings this week, we have seen how the word "bread" sometimes claims its literal meaning but frequently moves beyond that to embrace so much more: righteousness, forgiveness, acceptance, meaning, justice and peace, grace, salvation, the presence of Christ in the power of the Spirit. All these are facets of what is meant when we, the hungry, pray for "our daily bread." And yes, Jesus offers himself as the bread of life: "Take, eat. This is my body, given for you."

As our imaginations are stirred by the metaphorical applications of "bread," it is important to hear from the biblical prophets, too. We must remember that the literal meaning is never superseded. Providing real bread to the hungry remains an essential concern and calling for the people of God. We seek unity and community not least to provide a strong base for the work of mission, diakonia and the sharing of necessities.

Sharing. Sharing, too, is a key to Christian understanding. In teaching us to pray, our Lord does not suggest that each of us pray for "*my* daily bread." We pray for *our* daily bread, just as we address the prayer to *Our Father*.

During our group work, Daniel [Kirubaraj] made the point that in our communication we are called to show the links that bind together *God*, the believing *I*, and all the *neighbors* of those believing "I's." What I understand by this is that "God and I" is an insufficient relationship for a vibrant faith, even if the "I" includes the context of one's church community. The bread of heaven comes down to give life to the world, the whole world, including all those whom Christ teaches us to count as neighbors.

To hunger and thirst for righteousness is to recognize my neighbor's hunger as well as my own. In 1 Corinthians 10 and the *Didache*, the church of Jesus Christ is compared to *one* loaf containing many ingredients; the apostle Paul speaks of it as the one body of Christ, while the *Didache* sees it as the bread of the kingdom. Different means of communicating good news, different metaphors, are possible and may be deemed legitimate so long as we do not lose contact with the central touchstone of faith: the love of God in Jesus Christ brought to life among us through the work of the Holy Spirit.

It is also important for us to keep in mind that a loaf has no purpose by itself. Bread is meant to be blessed, broken and *given* to the imperfect so that we may be transformed, empowered and commissioned to ministries of reconciliation. Bread is to be offered to neighbors as well as shared among the family, for it is intended for all the world.

Christian communicators play a role in offering the bread of life to a hungry world. Ours is not the leading role, even within our churches, but we can make an impact on people's lives if only we maintain our focus on the good news of Jesus Christ, the bread of life, our daily bread for whom the world hungers.

And so we pray on our own behalf, and on behalf of all who are hungry "for acceptance, for righteousness and bread."

The answer to such prayers, I am happy to relate, has already been published:

> Blessed are those who hunger and thirst for righteousness, for they shall be satisfied. Amen.

* * *

From a hunger for that which does not satisfy, ***O Lord, deliver us.***
From words and deed that provoke divisions, prejudice and hatred, ***O Lord, deliver us.***
From all that prevents us from realizing your promises of peace and love, ***O Lord, deliver us.***
Save us from our brokenness, O Lord, and lead us into your kingdom.
Gib uns unser Brot für jeden Tag.
Give your people our daily bread, and grant that we may share it in love. Amen.

A Communicative Communion of Contextual and Mutual Sending

The Road to Communication Priorities

Message from the Consultation on Communication as a Mission and Ministry of the Church

Preamble

> ...We proclaim to you what we have seen and heard, so that you also may have fellowship with us. And our fellowship is with the Father and with his Son, Jesus Christ. We write this to make our joy complete.
>
> 1 John 1:3-4 (New International Version)

Communication of the good news in Jesus Christ has as its goal the broadening and deepening of *communio*, or Christian fellowship. And the community itself, as it rejoices, grows and matures, relies on authentic communication to maintain and strengthen the extended communion.

From its inception, the Church of Jesus Christ has been called to a ministry of the Word in which "we declare... what we have seen and heard" so that our audience may be inspired to "have fellowship with us." The Church's potential for communicating God's Word is revealed in the reported "tongues" of fire that appeared before believers on the day of Pentecost (Acts 2:3) when the Church began to communicate with miraculous clarity.

Martin Luther started one of his expositions of the Sermon on the Mount with commentary on the meaning of Matthew's introductory remark (5:2), "And he opened his mouth and taught them and spoke":[1]

---

[1] Jaroslav Pelikan, ed. and trans., *Luther's Work vol. 21: The Sermon on the Mount (Sermons) and the Magnificat* (St. Louis: Concordia Publishing House, 1956), 7.

> Here, the evangelist opens with a preface stating how Christ prepared
> Himself for the sermon he wanted to deliver: He went up on a mountain,
> sat down, and opened his mouth, to make it evident that he was in earnest.
> These are the three things, so to speak, which every good preacher should do:
> First, he takes his place; second, he opens his mouth and says something;
> third, he knows when to stop.

The skilled Christian communicator, in other words, is careful in planning both his content and strategy. Luther instructs anyone called to church office to speak "vigorously and confidently, to preach the truth that has been entrusted to him." A preacher who is muddled in message may speak many words, yet "he is not really opening his mouth."[2]

The church's mission of communication begins in the gift of the Word (John 1:1-14) and the recognition that the Triune God "has spoken to us" in Jesus Christ (Hebrews 1:2). This was attested by the apostles, who were commissioned as witnesses (Luke 24:48) and sent out to proclaim the good news (Matthew 28:19-20; Acts 1:8). The New Testament describes the proclamation (*kerygma*) of the divine Word (*Logos*) in the common words (*logoi*) of the people. This was not the sole means of communicating the gospel (for example, *diakonia, martyria, leitourgia* also won hearts and minds), but proclamation, interpretation and the writing of epistles, gospels and other early texts formed a key element in fostering community and resourcing evangelism.

The Lutheran World Federation (LWF) is a servant of the *communio* and of the Lord who has called us into fellowship. It is also a participant in the mission and ministry to which the church is called. Communication is foundational in the living out of the church's mission and ministry, and the LWF serves its churches and the larger ecumenical movement by facilitating an holistic approach to communication.

This document presents a vision of communication relevant to a family of churches concerned both for the pastoral and missional dimensions of fellowship. Ministry and mission belong to the core of our being as the body of Christ; the practice of skilled and caring communication is key to primary roles and offices of the church: prophecy, preaching, teaching, interpretation (Romans 12, 1 Corinthians 12, Ephesians 4).

As we contemplate the renewal of the LWF, we have an opportunity to reconsider the position of communication at the center of the *communio*. Renewal, like communication, affects the whole communion. For this reason, we have

---

[2] *Ibid.*, 9-10.

entrusted the creation of this preparatory document to experts in communication from a broadly representative sampling of our worldwide fellowship.

In June 2009 consultants on communication from a variety of churches
and ecumenical organizations were assembled at the Theological Faculty of
the Friedrich-Alexander University in Erlangen, Germany together with staff
members of LWF-Office for Communication Services and university professors
in the field of theology and communication. The presentations, conversations
and worship experiences of those days revolved around a theme inspired by
that of the Eleventh LWF Assembly: *Communication – Our Daily Bread: Communication as a Mission and Ministry of the Church.*

The background to our consultation arose from advance reading of the three
most recent documents related to communication in the LWF: the second draft
of *The Renewal Committee Report* (Arusha, 2008); *A Communicative Communion*
(LWF 2002) and *Mission in Context: Transformation, Reconciliation, Empowerment* (LWF 2004). An introductory presentation on the history of this aspect
of the LWF's work also reminded us of John W. Bachman's proposed vision
and ethic of honest interaction through open communication as outlined in
his paper: *A Constructive Contradiction?*

The consultation participants, from many churches and regions, sought an
understanding of communication that is both holistic and contextual, appropriate
to the transforming, reconciling and empowering mission of the Triune God. We
submit the following report as a contribution to the renewal of our communion.

Holistic: Sending and Communication

> … the good news can only be communicated effectively to people within their own
> context through language and actions which are an integral part of that context.[3]

This understanding of mission as accompaniment means encounter and communication for mutual understanding. The highest possible level of understanding
can only be reached by taking contexts into account, with mission following
a hermeneutical spiral.

Although communication is central to the mission—the sending—of the
church and is rooted in communication between God, humanity and the world,
there is no guarantee against misunderstandings in communication either

---

[3] *Mission in Context: Transformation, Reconciliation, Empowerment*, LWF, 2004, p. 8 in the online version
at **www.lutheranworld.org/LWF_Documents/EN/DMD-Mission-in-Context-low.pdf**

within the Lutheran communion or with ecumenical partners. It therefore needs to be seen as a highly professional discipline.

The essence of mission is to communicate life. In the Old Testament, the very essence of what is now called mission is sending: it is God who sends. This becomes even clearer in the New Testament: God sends Jesus; Jesus returns to God and sends the Holy Spirit to proclaim God's Kingdom and ask the people to glorify it in a life of worship. Forms of sending can be found in all four gospels, and we are reminded of that by the first sentences of the LWF document *A Communicative Communion*: "We are sending a strong message even when not saying anything. In our sleep, we also communicate. Communication is part and parcel of our very being, of life itself..."[4] Mission and communication together become sending. If not seen as being mission, communication must at the very least be seen as central to mission.

As sending is about incarnation, God enters into the totality of human existence,[5] and offers a model for holistic mission. Considering that communication is central to mission, communication must be holistic as well.

This means that everybody is involved. Communication is not just a profession, but equally about individuals and their personal stories. Together, they make attractive churches which are the source and outcome of effective sending.

In attempting to contribute to the development of an LWF communication policy, we will build on the three LWF documents cited above.

Understanding Communication

> Communication is a complex symbolic process whereby reality is produced, maintained, repaired and transformed.

Communication is intertwined with culture. Some consider that it leads or, at the very least, plays a dominating role in culture. Going deeper, communication is a basic human need and right and is also necessary for social cohesion. Its basic purpose is to make identity communicable. These last two statements indicate the basic nature of communication in relation to religion: communication is God's great gift to humanity. Leaving aside the "old" concept of communication as simply a process of transmission, we move into a "new" thinking: communication is a mutual process to build community. In relation to religion,

---

[4] *A Communicative Communion. LWF Guiding Principles for Comprehensive Communication.* LWF Draft, 2002, 2.

[5] *Mission in Context: Transformation, Reconciliation, Empowerment*, LWF, 2004, p. 26 in the online version at **www.lutheranworld.org/LWF_Documents/EN/DMD-Mission-in-Context-low.pdf**

communication assists in building a meaningful community, one which communicates accurately and in a timely manner in and through all levels.

This "new" thinking has emerged from changing views on the importance of audiences. Taking audiences into account immediately implies enabling communication in context, and reconsiders the tensions between transmission, proclamation and dialogue. Communication in context breaks new ground by revising the whole communication process and its relation with theology, including the church itself.

Communication and Context

Paul himself made use of audience-targeted, contextual communication:

> 1 Corinthians 9:19-23 (New International Version): [19]Though I am free and belong to no man, I make myself a slave to everyone, to win as many as possible. [20]To the Jews I became like a Jew, to win the Jews. To those under the law I became like one under the law (though I myself am not under the law), so as to win those under the law. [21]To those not having the law I became like one not having the law (though I am not free from God's law but am under Christ's law), so as to win those not having the law. [22]To the weak I became weak, to win the weak. I have become all things to all men so that by all possible means I might save some. [23]I do all this for the sake of the gospel, that I may share in its blessings.

Communicating in context does not automatically imply that every cultural context can be rendered understandable in other contexts through communication. Yet, although it is not possible to translate all communication in a way that everyone understands, contextual culture can be shared and useful for intercultural communication.

Studies of culture and context tend more or less to agree on how different cultures can communicate. A useful analogy compares the system of culture to that of a many-layered onion. Its core contains the basic values. This core can scarcely be modified. The surrounding layers consist (from the inside out) of rituals, heroes and symbols. As one moves from the layers closest to the core to those further out, it becomes easier to change, syncretize, adopt or consider different rituals, heroes or symbols. The three outer layers together are the practices of a group, the flexible part. This is why groups are able to live with one another and adjust to the society they are in.

Transposing this to the Lutheran communion, theology is an explicit articulation of a perspective in two ways. It is an articulation of faith in a given belief system, but it is also an articulation of lived practices in a cultural setting. Being aware of the differences, and of the fact that both are necessary in communication, cements the need for communication to deal with all the different cultural layers.

All of this implies that communication can and should be holistic, and that this needs to be a foundational priority for communication practices within the LWF communion.

Communication as a Mission and Ministry: A Communicative Communion of Contextual and Mutual Sending

An Explicit Call for Independent Christian Journalism

Before making recommendations, participants at the Erlangen consultation on "Communication as a Mission and Ministry: A Communicative Communion of Contextual and Mutual Sending" wished to issue an explicit and urgent call for independent Christian journalism. Based on the understanding of communication set out above, they felt that independent Christian journalism plays a major role in enabling freedom in Christianity and in honing the churches' capacities for mission. Independent journalism, they said, secures the continuity of the freedom of the gospel.

The Road to Communication Priorities

Practical Applications: How to Do Communication

In an effort to explore the "how to" of communication and taking into account all the above-mentioned considerations, we have identified a number of very practical key approaches to how to communicate within the LWF. The following recommendations evoke in note form how we see our respective communication roles in our own contexts at different levels within the LWF communion, and also what we feel will assist and enable our future work in this area.

Global Level

The role of the LWF Office for Communication Services (OCS) is to:

- enable the sharing of life resources, experiences and information;

- celebrate creation, local successes and failures as a proof of real and possible communion, telling/celebrating the stories of our member churches using people as resources;
- assist in identifying church practices that might be useful to others and investigate opportunities for a communication/communicators' competition, identifying and sharing best communication practices, creating a database or "communal garden" to document and share these projects;
- foster an environment that allows for the exchange of best practices;
- develop opportunities for communication training;
- invite participation from all LWF members;
- recognize that while new technology is critical to the work of LWF-OCS, we cannot lose sight of more traditional communication media including drama, writing, songs—all of which can be used to promote the Lutheran communion;
- highlight and favor human relationships, contacts, visits;
- validate the necessity for independent journalism (in cooperation with the World Association for Christian Communication – WACC); reaffirm the role of outlets such as *Ecumenical News International* (*ENI*);
- recognize a role for communication in documenting the history of church events and activities; encourage regional communication officers to help write the history of their churches;
- foster integrity within church journalism;
- share encounters and involvement between members of the communion and examples of sharing in the life and the worship of member churches;
- conceive and implement communication activities ecumenically.

National and Regional Levels

The following recommendations and resolutions came out of our discussion on the role of communication within LWF member churches. They reveal something of the national contexts in which the churches carry out their communication and mission tasks, and show the diversity of the various church cultures.

India / Asia

- Create a communication group, bringing the values of the kingdom of God, the gospel of life-sharing and life-saving
- Provide an information service
- Underline the importance of family values

Latvia

- Be the voice of the church
- Make the church visible
- Make the message of the church heard, but also help church members, particularly grassroots members, to communicate and assist them in their evangelizing role
- Create unity

Brazil

- Create unity by underlining what is in common
- Share the good things we are doing and find forums for dialogue

Nigeria

- Bridge the gap between the congregation and the hierarchy, connect the local church to the regional and global church
- As communicators be effective resource persons and focus on the best media for local settings

USA (Presbyterian Church)

- The budget line used for pastors and a newspaper is now used for an online magazine disseminating its news to pastors electronically
- The communication office's work is the information source about the church
- Local assistance, education and training for communicators are needed

Canada

- Being a public voice
- Telling the stories of the church
- Sharing information
- Being a bridge (from global to local and vice versa)

Thoughts for Consideration When Prioritizing

As far as resources are concerned, expression of the communion needs to be considered in context. In some regions, it may make sense to invest in radio or mobile phone outreach rather than putting resources into publishing. In others, most people have no access to new technology while in yet others, this is the ideal way to reach new audiences. Currently accessible resources, including those that could be shared between different churches and regions, should be identified.

At the same time, we need to re-evaluate what is "on the ground" and identify those communication projects that are really meeting our needs as well as those where alternatives are needed.

Within the communion, there are roles for communicators at the global, regional and national levels. All must play an active role in articulating and implementing the communication strategy for LWF, "recognizing that we are part of a communion, we are not just receivers, but contributors as well."

Other key factors to consider when planning for effective LWF communication include

- how people receive our communication;
- how it affects family and community;
- communication levels;
- local churches/congregations as focal points of new (and old) media and as media resource centers; and also
- making a contribution to/finding a voice in the independent, secular media (in order to support media integrity in society);
- uncharted risks in the new media.

The Role of Communication Within the LWF Communion

The four main tasks for communication within the LWF communion are: to create unity, to play a bridging role, to allow the sharing of faith experiences, and to share resources.

In its role of furthering *unity*, communication within the communion should bring together global and regional offices and member churches, taking into account not only the differences between them but also what unites them. It should focus on the call and mission of the church, and highlight the Bible as a common point of reference.

Communication within the communion should also play a bridging role between the LWF's different regional expressions, and between the church and people outside it. As far as the latter is concerned, communication needs to analyze people's communication habits—"Where are the people and where do they communicate?" It should be open and ready for dialogue and communication, finding opportunities to connect people with the church.

From the grassroots to the global level, communication should help identify new opportunities to help bridge the technical divide, and share different faith experiences, mission approaches, resources and advocacy.

It should also encourage, empower and share resources. In the spirit of being in communion from grassroots to global levels, communication brings people together to share and lift up best practices. It should help create pilot projects—like the "Communio Garden" —that move communication from interpretation to being and becoming expressions of communion.

Setting Communication Priorities Within the LWF

In view of the significance of communication in the light of contextual and mutual sending, organizing from the bottom up is the basis of communication priorities. Communication is meant to reach the place where the church is—which is where the people are.

"Since mission is contextual and is carried out by every church in every place, local congregations play a crucial role, especially in developing resources for mission."[6] Between the local and global, levels of communication need to be taken into account, communication gaps reduced, and sharing and caring relationships maintained.

The following questions need to be asked when setting LWF communication priorities; our discussion lifted up some of the following responses.

Why communicate? The LWF must communicate because "there is no communion without communication," "we care," "we want to proclaim the gospel," "we want to share and strengthen Lutheran identity." Within a given context, this sense of identity will be based, among other things, on shared values, on the presence and status of other confessions, faiths and beliefs, on shared social activities (like membership of a church choir)...

With whom? The targets of LWF communication are "everyone in the communion and everyone we care for," "congregations, churches and church bodies," "local communities," "the secular world"; communication between these target groups needs to be facilitated.

What do we need to know? People communicate well when they are using the means available in their own societies, at the most reasonable cost. For effective communication, the means available in various LWF contexts and, if

---

[6] *Mission in Context: Transformation, Reconciliation, Empowerment*, LWF, 2004, p. 56 in the online version at **www.lutheranworld.org/LWF_Documents/EN/DMD-Mission-in-Context-low.pdf**

necessary, their relative cost efficiency, need to be investigated and the digital divide overcome.

What methods/tools can we use? Mapping communication resources—of the Lutheran communion, of other ecumenical and non-ecumenical resources and of communication projects—is a helpful tool for effective communication. Other useful methods include SWOT analysis, and development of communication priorities for the communion.

A Final Remark for the Communicator

Rev. Theodore Gill offered the following evening prayer during the consultation:

> One does not live by bread alone, but by every word that comes from the mouth of God.

Not *every* word proceeds from the mouth of God; even words of Holy Scripture may be twisted to demonic uses, to satanic uses. "Come along," Satan entices, "throw yourself from this height – for *it is written* that God will give the angels charge over you, and they will not let you be bruised." In the present instance, though, Satan employs logic rather than proof-texts: (1) God gives you power to turn stones to bread; (2) You are hungry, and surrounded by stones; (3) There-fore…? It is a straightforward syllogism. (Deuteronomy 8:3, Matthew 4:1-4)

But Jesus rejects this word, this logic, because he knows the speaker. He is fasting as a means of seeking a word that comes from the mouth of God; nothing less will do. Satan's argument shows sophistication in its logic, a feigned respect in its appreciation of what Jesus is able to do. "Take the bread you need. Put your talent to work. Use the raw material at hand."

Jesus is looking for something even more basic than bread. At first glance, fasting may seem contradictory to the prayer for daily bread, but this is what one of our speakers has cited as "constructive contradiction." In his commit-ment to fasting and his quest for the proper word, Jesus doubts Satan's concern for human well-being. He finds the devil's advice to be anything *but* "credible communication."

This is still a very early moment in our consultation, but the text on Christ's temptation in the wilderness may suggest one provisional conclusion: words and other vehicles of communication are not valuable in themselves. Even Satan can quote the Bible. Not just any "bread" will do, no matter how hungry we are. There may be a case for "art for art's sake," but: *No* to communion for communion's sake alone. *No* to communication for communication's sake.

The value of communication is no mere matter of reason or sophistication, or of utilizing particular systems and processes in disseminating a message. More important is the heart of the messenger and the consequence of the words.

List of Contributors

Rev. Karin **Achtelstetter** of the Evangelical Lutheran Church in Bavaria is the director and editor-in-chief of the LWF Office of Communication Services (OCS).

Ms Brenda V. **Akpan** of the Lutheran Church of Nigeria is the chairperson of the LWF Program Committee for World Service and editor of the Africa Lutheran Communication and Information Network (ALCINET). She is pursuing doctoral studies at the University of Basel's Institute for Social Anthropology and Centre for African Studies.

Ms Praxedis **Bouwman** of the Protestant Church in the Netherlands is the president of the Communication Committee of Lutheran Minority Churches in Europe (KALME) and vice-president of the World Association for Christian Communication (WACC).

Ms Trina **Gallop** of the Evangelical Lutheran Church in Canada (ELCIC) is the director of Communications and Stewardship in the ELCIC.

Rev. Theodore **Gill** of the Presbyterian Church (USA) is the senior editor of World Council of Churches (WCC) Publications in Geneva.

Prof. Johanna **Haberer** of the Evangelical Lutheran Church in Bavaria is an ordained minister of her church, professor of Christian Communication and vice president of the Friedrich Alexander University in Erlangen, Germany.

Mr Jaime **Jung** of the Evangelical Church of the Lutheran Confession in Brazil is a PhD student in Christian Communication at the Theological Faculty of the Friedrich Alexander University in Erlangen, Germany.

Mr Peter **Kenny** is the editor-in-chief of *Ecumenical News International* (*ENI*).

Rev. Dr Daniel **Kirubaraj** of the United Evangelical Lutheran Church in India (UELCI) is a pastor of the Arcot Lutheran Church in Chennai, India.

Mr Ivars **Kupcis** of the Evangelical Lutheran Church of Latvia (ELCL) is a member of the ELCL Public Relations Commission.

Ms Elizabeth **Lobulu** of the Evangelical Lutheran Church in Tanzania (ELCT) is the ELCT communications coordinator and *Lutheran World Information* (*LWI*) African region editor.

Prof. Dr Andreas **Nehring** is an ordained minister of the Evangelical Lutheran Church in Bavaria and chair of the Department of Christian Mission and Religious Studies at the Friedrich Alexander University in Erlangen, Germany.